Learn Advanced Spanish for Adults Workbook

Go from Spanish Intermediate to Advanced in 30 Days!

Table of Contents

Introduction

Chapter 1: I Am What I Am _____ *1*

Chapter 2: Careers _____ *21*

Chapter 3: Anecdotes and Gossip _____ *43*

Chapter 4: Protecting the Environment _____ *65*

Chapter 5: Online and Offline Relationships _____ *84*

Conclusion _____ *106*

Introduction

Are you looking for a simple book that will help you achieve fluency in Spanish? Well, look no further because this book was definitely made for you. Whether you are an intermediate Spanish student or you know a lot of Spanish but want to learn how to talk like a true native, ***Learn Advanced Spanish for Adults Workbook: Go from Spanish Intermediate to Advanced in 30 Days!*** will help you achieve the fluency you're looking for!

This book doesn't simply focus on grammar and structures, but it also focuses on different conversation topics in order to learn a lot of advanced new vocabulary, expressions and set phrases.

You will find that learning Spanish doesn't have to be that difficult! You really can get to an advanced level of Spanish with this book. Your 30 days start **today**! *¡Empecemos!*

Chapter 1: I Am What I Am

Descubre quién eres, pero no te aferres a ninguna definición. Muta las veces que sea necesario para vivir en la totalidad de tu ser.

- Claudio Naranjo

Hey! We're about to start our 30-day Spanish learning journey. *¿Estás listo?¡Comencemos!*

Parts of the Body

We will divide the body into sections to later talk about each part in that section, and we will see each part of the body with its corresponding article and English translation. Let's find out what we're made of in Spanish!

*En **la cabeza** tenemos...* ("In the head, we have...")

- *La cara* ("face")
- *Los ojos* ("eyes")
- *Los párpados* ("eyelids")
- *Las pestañas* ("eyelashes")
- *Las cejas* ("brow")
- *La nariz* ("nose")
- *La boca* ("mouth")
- *Los labios* ("lips")
- *Los dientes* ("teeth")

- *Las orejas* ("ears")
- *Las mejillas* ("cheeks")
- *La frente* ("forehead")
- *El mentón* ("chin")
- *El pelo* ("hair")
- *El cabello* ("hair")
- *La nuca* ("nape")
- *El cuello* ("neck")

En **el torso** *tenemos...* ("In the trunk, we have...")

- *El pecho* ("chest")
- *Los hombros* ("shoulders")
- *La espalda* ("back")
- *Los abdominales* ("abs")
- *La panza* ("tummy"): used in some Spanish-speaking countries
- *La barriga* ("tummy"): used in other Spanish-speaking countries
- *El estómago* ("stomach")
- *El ombligo* ("navel")
- *La cintura* ("waist")
- *La cadera* ("hip")

En **los brazos,** *tenemos...* ("In the arms, we have...")

- *El codo* ("elbow")
- *El antebrazo* ("forearm")
- *La muñeca* ("wrist")
- *La mano* ("hand")
- *La palma de la mano* ("palm of the hand")
- *Los dedos* ("fingers")
  - *El pulgar* ("thumb")
  - *El índice* ("index finger")

- ○ *El dedo corazón or medio* ("middle finger")
- ○ *El dedo anular* ("ring finger")
- ○ *El meñique* ("little finger")
- *Los nudillos* ("knuckles")

*En **las piernas**, tenemos...* ("In the legs, we have...")

- *El muslo* ("thigh")
- *La rodilla* ("knee")
- *El tobillo* ("ankle")
- *El pie* ("foot")
- *Los dedos del pie* ("toes")
- *El talón* ("heel")
- *La planta del pie* ("sole")

*Los **órganos vitales** son...* ("The vital organs are...")

- *El cerebro* ("brain")
- *El corazón* ("heart")
- *Los pulmones* ("lungs")
- *El hígado* ("liver")
- *Los intestinos* ("intestines")
- *Los riñones* ("kidneys")

Illnesses and Pains

If we simply want to say that something hurts, we use the verb *doler*. For example: *Me duelen los pies*. The verb *doler* works similarly to the verb *gustar* in this case, since we use the singular *(duele)* or plural *(duelen)* forms depending on the number of the part of the body that hurts, and we use the same pronouns that we use with *gustar* (*me, te, le, nos, os, les*). So, in contrast to *Me duelen los pies*, we could have something like *Me duele la cabeza*.

Additionally, there are optional elements you can include. For example, if someone told us *"Me duelen los pies,"* we could answer *"A mí no me duelen los pies."* In this way, by including the *a mí* in our sentence and stressing it a bit in our speech; we are saying that, despite the fact that the other person's feet hurt, ours do not!

Of course, at this level we can also add the reason why something hurts with *por, porque* and even *de*. Let's see some examples:

- *Me duelen los pies por caminar mucho*. ("My feet hurt from walking a lot")
- *Me duelen los pies porque caminé mucho*. ("My feet hurt because I walked a lot")
- *Me duelen los pies de tanto caminar*. ("My feet hurt from so much walking")

Notice that with *por* and *de*, the reason must be in the infinitive, while with *porque* it should be conjugated.

To say that something hurts, we can also talk about the noun *el dolor*, which means "the pain" and can be used to say that you feel pain somewhere with the verbs *sentir* or *tener*. For example:

- *Siento dolor en el pecho*. ("I feel pain in my chest")
- *Sientes dolor en las manos*. ("You feel pain in your hands")
- *Tiene dolor de espalda*. ("He has back pain")
- *Tenemos dolor de pies*. ("We have feet pain")

Notice that, in these examples, we can see that with *sentir dolor* we use the preposition *en* followed by the part of the body with the article before. However, with *tener dolor*, we usually use the preposition *de* followed by the part of the body without the article.

We could also have difficulties doing things. To express this, we could use the verb *tener* with the noun *dificultad*, which means "difficulty," or we could use the verb *costar*, which means "to have a hard time doing something". Let's see some examples of this:

- *Tengo dificultad para caminar.* ("I have difficulty walking")
- *Tengo dificultad para levantar el brazo.* ("I have difficulty lifting my arm")
- *Me cuesta mover la pierna.* ("I have a hard time moving my leg")
- *Me cuesta levantarme.* ("I have a hard time standing up")

In this case, with both *tener dificultad* and *costar,* we use verbs in the infinitive. With *tener dificultad*, though, we should always have the preposition *para* before the infinitive verb.

Now it's time to talk about some common illnesses and symptoms. Actually, the phrases we've seen so far could be used to talk about symptoms like *dolor de cabeza*, right? But in this case, we will be dealing with some nouns!

- *La gripe* ("the flu")
- *El resfriado* ("cold")
- *La alergia* ("allergy")
- *La fractura* ("fracture" or "break")
- *La migraña* ("migraine")
- *Las náuseas* ("nausea" or "sickness")
- *La ansiedad* ("anxiety")
- *La tos* ("cough")
- *Los estornudos* ("sneezes")
- *La fiebre* ("fever")

But how do we use these nouns? Well, with these nouns we use the verb *tener*. Let's see how that would be:

- *Tengo gripe.* ("I have the flu")
- *Tengo un resfriado.* ("I have a cold")
- *Tengo alergia.* ("I have allergies")
- *Tengo una fractura en la pierna* ("I have a fracture in my leg")
- *Tengo migraña* ("I have a migraine")
- *Tengo náuseas* ("I have nausea")
- *Tengo ansiedad* ("I have anxiety")
- *Tengo tos* ("I have a cough")
- *Tengo fiebre* ("I have a fever")

Notice that only with *resfriado* we use an article, but it's more common to use *resfriado* and *resfriada* as adjectives with the verb *estar*: *Estoy resfriado/a*. You should also note that we didn't include *estornudos* in our examples. Well, just like in English, in Spanish we don't usually say "*Tengo estornudos.*" We generally use the verb *estornudar*. However, *estornudar* isn't the only one that can actually be a verb. *Fracturar* ("to break") and *toser* ("to cough") are also verbs we can use instead of the noun. Let's see some examples:

- *He estado <u>estornudando</u> todo el día* ("I've been sneezing all day")
- *¡<u>Estornudó</u> 20 veces seguidas!* ("She sneezed 20 times in a row!")
- *Me <u>fracturé</u> la pierna cuando jugaba al fútbol.* ("I broke my leg while playing football")
- *Mi hijo se <u>fracturó</u> el brazo ayer.* ("My son broke his arm yesterday")
- *¿Te duele el pecho cuando toses?* ("Does your chest hurt when you cough?")
- *<u>Toso</u> mucho por las mañanas.* ("I cough a lot in the mornings")

Now, what if we go to the doctor and talk about our illnesses, symptoms, and the things that hurt? Well, the doctor might give you one of the following recommendations:

- *Hacer reposo* ("To rest")
- *Descansar* ("To rest")
- *Tomar medicinas* ("To take medicine")
    - *Tomar analgésicos* ("To take painkillers")
    - *Tomar anti inflamatorios* ("To take anti-inflammatory drugs")
    - *Tomar un jarabe* ("To take a syrup")
- *Ponerse un yeso* ("To get a cast")
- *Hacer estudios* ("To run some tests")

Now, let's see everything we've learned so far in the following text message that Carlos sent to Mariana because he couldn't attend her birthday party:

¡Hola, Mariana! Lamento no haber podido ir a tu fiesta anoche. Hacía ya unos días que me dolía la pierna y no le di importancia. Pero ayer me costaba moverme del dolor, así que fui al médico. Me hizo algunos estudios y me dijo que me había fracturado. ¿Puedes creerlo? ¡Y yo no lo sabía! Me dijo que tomara unos analgésicos para el dolor de pierna, me puso un yeso y me recomendó hacer reposo por diez días.

Feelings and Moods

So far, you've surely learned how to talk about your feelings with the verb *estar* or the verb *sentirse*, which means "to feel," followed by many different adjectives that you might already know. For example: *triste, enojado, feliz, contento,* etc. But now we're going to focus on a different (and more complex) way to express our feelings.

Sentirse + Set Expressions

We can use the verb *sentirse* with some set expressions. *Sentirse* is also a verb that requires a pronoun, but it doesn't work like *gustar* and *doler* because *sentirse* doesn't require an indirect object. *Sentirse* is actually a reflexive verb, which means that it requires a reflexive pronoun. Luckily, reflexive pronouns are almost the same as the indirect object pronouns that *gustar* and *doler* require, they are: *me, te, se, nos, os, se* (while the indirect object pronouns are: *me, te, le, nos, os, les*). The main difference between verbs like *gustar* and *doler* and reflexive verbs is that reflexive verbs do need to be conjugated in all the different persons and numbers, while verbs like *gustar* and *doler* only change from plural to singular depending on the number of the direct object.

Let's have a look at the following table to refresh our memories on how reflexive pronouns work!

(Subject Pronoun)	Reflexive Pronoun	Sentir
(yo)	me	siento
(tú)	te	sientes
(él / ella / usted)	se	siente
(nosotros / nosotras)	nos	sentimos
(vosotros / vosotras)	os	sentís
(ellos / ellas / ustedes)	se	sienten

When looking at this table, you should bear in mind that the verb *sentir* is actually an irregular verb in the present indicative. You must have noticed it because of the way its root changes from *sen-* to *sien-* in some cases!

It's time to have a look at the way *sentirse* works with some set phrases and their meanings!

- *Sentirse fuera de lugar*: to feel out of place
- *Sentirse como en casa*: to feel at home
- *Sentirse como pez en el agua*: to feel like fish in water
- *Sentirse como sapo de otro pozo:* to feel like fish out of water
- *Sentirse eufórico/a:* to feel elated
- *Sentirse a gusto*: to feel comfortable
- *Sentirse con/sin ánimos*: to feel in high/low spirits
- *Sentirse con vigor/fuerzas*: to feel vigorous
- *Sentirse como un/a niño/a*: to feel like a child

Describing People

As we already know, we can use the verb *ser* followed by an adjective to describe someone. But there are other ways of describing people's personality.

Adjectives to Describe People

Let's see a few adjectives that you probably haven't seen before!

- glotón/*a*: glutton
- *Hablador/a*: talkative, funny, eloquent
- *parlanchín/a*: talkative
- *enamoradizo/a*: who falls in love easily
- *fantasioso/a*: day-dreamer
- *flojo/a*: lazy
- *vago/a*: lazy
- *seco/a*: lacks empathy, unfriendly
- *sieso/a*: nasty, unpleasant, unfriendly

- *soso/a*: ungracious
- *empalagoso/a*: affectionate
- *despreocupado*: indifferent about important things
- *tolerante*: tolerant
- *flexible*: flexible
- *quisquilloso/a*: meticulous, picky
- *dedicado/a*: dedicated
- *meticuloso/a*: meticulous
- *caótico/a*: chaotic
- *decidido/a*: determined, decisive
- *indeciso/a*: indecisive
- *tranquilo/a*: quiet, calm
- *inquieto/a*: anxious, restless
- *exigente*: demanding
- *estricto/a*: strict
- *maniático/a*: manic
- *sensato/a*: sensible, wise
- *metódico/a*: methodical
- *desordenado/a*: untidy
- *relajado/a*: relaxed
- *tenso/a*: tense
- *maduro/a*: mature
- *hiperactivo/a*: hyperactive
- *simple*: simple

Reflejar/Mostrar la Personalidad

First, based on some kind of evidence, we can use the phrases *reflejar su personalidad* or *mostrar su personalidad* followed by an adjective to talk about how some actions or things reflect someone's personality. Let's see some examples:

- *El escritorio de Juana está muy ordenado, <u>refleja su personalidad metódica.</u>* ("Juana's desk is very tidy, it reflects her methodical personality.")
- *El andar lento de Ignacio y Paula <u>refleja su personalidad tranquila.</u>* ("Ignacio's slow walking reflects his calm personality.")
- *La vestimenta casual y la mochila de Pedro <u>muestran su personalidad flexible</u> como jefe.* ("Pedro's casual clothing and backpack show his flexible personality as a boss.")
- *Mi peinado elegante <u>muestra mi personalidad quisquillosa.</u>* ("My elegant hairstyle shows my meticulous personality.")

Remember that with these phrases the possessive adjective *su* needs to change depending on who we're talking about.

Moreover, note that the subject of these sentences is the "evidence" (Juana's desk, Ignacio and Paula's walking, Pedro's clothing and backpack, and my hairstyle), and that's the reason why the verbs *reflejar* and *mostrar* are in the singular when that subject is singular (like in the case of Juana's desk and my hairstyle) or in the infinitive (like in the case of Ignacio and Paula's walking) and plural when the subject is plural (like in the case of Pedro's clothing and backpack). Therefore, to decide whether the verb is singular or plural, the number of people we're talking about isn't relevant, it is only relevant to determine the possessive adjective we'll use.

Propio de/Típico de

Another way of talking about people's personality based on some kind of evidence is using the phrase *propio de* or *típico de*... These phrases mean "proper of" and "typical of" and we can use them to say that a certain attitude or behavior is a characteristic of someone with a certain personality trait. Let's see some examples:

- *La forma de trabajar de Sandra es <u>propia de una persona decidida</u>.* ("Sandra's way of working is proper of a decided person.")

-

- *¿Has oído la respuesta de Paula? Su forma de hablar es <u>típica de una persona seca</u>.* ("Have you heard Paula's answer? Her way of talking is typical of an unfriendly person.")

The gender and number of the adjectives *propio* and *típico* depend on the gender and number of the subject (*la forma de trabajar de Sandra, tus hábitos alimenticios, su forma de hablar,* and *el horario de Luciano*). Before the phrases *propio de* and *típico de,* we always use the verb *ser* in its corresponding conjugation. After these phrases we use the nouns *una persona* or (*las*) *personas* depending on whether we want to talk about people in general using the singular or the plural. If we decide to use the plural form, we can choose between using the article *las* or leaving it out, but we cannot dispose of the article *una* when we use the singular form. Finally, after *persona* or *personas,* we should add the adjective that describes the personality trait we mean to say. This adjective, of course, should agree in gender and number with *persona* or *personas.*

Fama and *Imagen*

First, let's talk about the phrases with *fama*: *Tener fama de...* and *Ganarse fama de...* which could be translated as "Have a reputation for..." and "Gain a reputation for..." Let's see some examples:

- *¿Has oído que Carolina será la nueva jefa? <u>Tiene fama de ser muy exigente</u>.* ("Have you heard that Caroline will be the new boss? She has a reputation for being strict.")

-

- *Fernando se ha ganado la fama de empalagoso, cuando vino con su novia nunca se alejó de su lado.* ("Fernando gained a reputation for being affectionate, when he came with his girlfriend he never left her side.")
- *Me he ganado fama de enamoradizo por enamorarme de cuatro personas en un año.* ("I've gained a reputation for falling in love easily because I fell in love with four people within a year.")

With the phrase *"Tener fama de,"* we don't usually add any article before *fama.* However, with *"Ganarse fama de,"* we can choose to add the indefinite article *una* or even the definite article *la,* or have no article at all.

Then we have a phrase with *imagen,* which refers to the image people project of themselves. We can actually use the phrase *"Proyectar una imagen de..."* to express precisely that. Let's see it in use!

- *Gloria proyecta una imagen de persona estricta, pero no lo es para nada. Creo que tiene que ver con su postura.* ("Gloria projects an image of a strict person, but she isn't at all. I think it has to do with her posture.")
- *Lorenzo duerme mucho y por eso proyecta una imagen de persona vaga.* ("Lorenzo sleeps a lot and that's why he projects an image of a lazy person.")

As you can see, just like with *propio de* and *típico de,* we use the noun *persona* in these phrases. We can simply add the noun *persona* and an adjective right after it to express what the person's image projects. With this phrase, we can also use nouns that express what we mean directly after the preposition *de.* Let's see some examples of this!

- *Karen proyecta una imagen de tranquilidad cada vez que habla.* ("Karen projects an image of peace every time she talks.")

- *Federico es tan caótico que a veces <u>proyecta una imagen de confusión</u>.* ("Federico is so chaotic that he projects an image of confusion.")

Now let's have a look at this conversation between two colleagues, Julio (●) and Lila (○), who are talking about a new colleague (Manuela).

● Lila, ¿Ya has trabajado con Manuela?

○ No, pero ya se ha ganado la fama de floja.

● ¿De verdad? Pues yo acabo de trabajar con ella y me pareció muy dedicada.

○ Puede ser que tengas razón. Pasé por su escritorio y creo que refleja una personalidad quisquillosa. ¡Todo está en perfecto orden!

● Apuesto que sí, un escritorio ordenado es típico de alguien así. Además tenía actitudes propias de una persona trabajadora. No creo que sea vaga.

○ Puede que tengas razón o quizás es floja pero proyecta una imagen de meticulosa.

● Pues no lo creo, parecía genuina, pero aún no la conozco bien.

○ Supongo que lo averiguaremos.

Exercises

1. Parts of the body
   a. In Spanish, name five things we have in our *cara*.
   b. In Spanish, name three things we have in our *torso*.
   c. In Spanish, name at least 2 *dedos*.
   d. In Spanish, name at least 3 *órganos vitales*.

2. Fill in the gaps with *duele/duelen* or *por/porque/de*
   a. Me .... la cabeza .... ayer tomé mucho alcohol.
   b. A mi hermano le .... los brazos .... hacer ejercicio.
   c. A Carla y Diego ya les .... el cerebro .... tanto pensar.
   d. Hace unos días me corté la punta de estos dos dedos, pero ya no me .... ya se curaron.

3. Fill in the gaps with the right conjugation of *sentir* or *tener*.
   a. Hace ya algunos días que Marcela .... dolor de espalda.
   b. Paola y Luis no vendrán hoy, los dos .... dolor de espalda de tanto ejercitar.
   c. Ernesto y yo .... dolor en el pecho. ¿Tú también?
   d. ¿Aún .... dolor de garganta? Hace 2 semanas que estás resfriada, deberías ir al médico.

4. Decide whether you should fill the gaps with the preposition *para* or with nothing at all.
   a. Lucía tiene dificultad .... respirar por las noches.

    b. A Santiago le cuesta .... mover la rodilla.

    c. ¿Si a ustedes les cuesta .... bailar y mover la cadera, qué me queda a mí con 78 años?

    d. Mis padres ya son grandes y tienen dificultad .... levantarse del sillón.

5. Complete the set phrases according to the definition:
    a. Sentirse ....: when you feel that you don't belong somewhere or with a group of people.
    b. Sentirse ....: to feel very happy.
    c. Sentirse ....: to feel sad and unhappy and not wanting to do anything.

6. Complete the following sentences with the phrases from the box

> esa incertidumbre de no saber qué sucederá - ese sentirse como en casa con la otra persona - ese dolor de espalda cada vez que te levantas de la cama - ese saber que has hecho un buen trabajo

    a. Estar en pareja es ....
    b. Ser ascendido en el trabajo es ....
    c. Ser despedido es ....
    d. Llegar a viejo es ....

7. Complete the following sentences with a form of the phrases *reflejar/mostrar su personalidad* and a corresponding adjective from the box below. Remember to make the adjectives agree in number with the people we're talking about.

> relajada - desordenada - inquieta - fantasiosa

    a. ¿Has oído el plan de Luisa? ¡Es una locura! ¡Es imposible hacer todo eso! Su plan definitivamente ....

b. Diego y Valeria ni siquiera prepararon el plan que les pedimos. Dicen que las cosas saldrán bien sin un plan. Eso ....

c. Bueno, vuestro plan .... porque comienza por la mitad, luego llega al final, vuelve a la mitad y por último termina en el principio.

d. Por último está mi plan. Ya sé que .... porque no solo hice el plan sino que ya hice los preparativos y no pude dormir en toda la noche pensando en eso.

8. Can you now replace the sentences with *reflejar/mostrar su personalidad* from the previous exercise for phrases with *propio/típico de* that have the same meaning?

9. Fill in the gaps with the right form of the phrases *tener fama de, ganarse fama de*, or *proyectar una imagen de*.
    a. Por su vestido, sus uñas arregladas y su cabello, Florencia .... persona quisquillosa.
    b. Mis tías .... parlanchinas, pero yo creo que no es cierto.
    c. Después de que ocasionaron ese lío en el trabajo, vosotras .... caóticas.

10. Read the following text and answer the questions below. Cuando Felicia comenzó a trabajar en esta empresa, se ganó fama de vaga, pero nadie supo por qué. Todos comenzaron a juzgarla por eso, pero nadie la conocía. Por eso, Felicia se sentía como sapo de otro pozo en la empresa y sin ánimos de nada. Intentó vestirse diferente y hacerse diferentes peinados para proyectar una imagen de persona dedicada, pero no funcionó. Después de un mes, su trabajo real comenzó a reflejar su personalidad profesional, decidida, trabajadora y divertida y

todos dejaron de pensar que era vaga. Por fin, Felicia se comenzó a sentir como pez en el agua en la empresa y, para ella, trabajar se convirtió en ese disfrutar de todos los días.

a. ¿Felicia se ganó fama de empalagosa?
b. ¿Felicia se sentía fuera de lugar en la empresa al comienzo?
c. ¿Qué intentó Felicia para cambiar su fama?
d. ¿Cuándo comenzó a reflejar su personalidad real?
e. Cuando todo terminó, Felicia se sintió...
   i. Eufórica
   ii. Con fuerzas
   iii. Sin ánimos
   iv. Como una niña

Answer Key

1.

   a. Options: *ojos, párpados, pestañas, cejas, nariz, boca, labios, dientes, mejillas, frente, mentón*

   b. Options: *pecho, hombros, espalda, abdominales, panza/barriga, estómago, ombligo, cintura, cadera*

   c. Option: *pulgar, índice, dedo corazón or medio, dedo anular, meñique*

   d. Option: *cerebro, corazón, pulmones, hígado, intestinos, riñones*

2.

   a. Me <u>duele</u> la cabeza <u>porque</u> ayer tomé mucho alcohol.

   b. A mi hermano le <u>duelen</u> los brazos <u>de/por</u> hacer ejercicio.

   c. A Carla y Diego ya les <u>duele</u> el cerebro <u>de/por</u> tanto pensar.

   d. Hace unos días me corté la punta de estos dos dedos, pero ya no me <u>duelen</u> <u>porque</u> ya se curaron.

3.

   a. siente/tiene

   b. sienten/tienen

   c. sentimos/tenemos

   d. sientes/tienes

4.

   a. para

   b. -

   c. -

   d. Para

5.

   a. como sapo de otro pozo

   b. eufórico

   c. sin ánimos

6.
   a. ese sentirse como en casa con la otra persona
   b. ese saber que has hecho un buen trabajo
   c. esa incertidumbre de no saber qué sucederá
   d. ese dolor de espalda cada vez que te levantas de la cama

7.
   a. muestra/refleja su personalidad fantasiosa
   b. muestra/refleja sus personalidades relajadas
   c. muestra/refleja vuestras personalidades desordenadas
   d. muestra/refleja mi personalidad inquieta

8.
   a. Propio/típico de una persona fantasiosa
   b. Propio/típico de (las) personas relajadas
   c. Propio/típico de (las) personas desordenadas
   d. Propio/típico de una persona inquieta

9.
   a. proyecta una imagen de
   b. tienen fama de
   c. os ganasteis fama de

10.
   a. No, de vaga/floja.
   b. Sí.
   c. Intentó vestirse diferente y hacerse diferentes peinados.
   d. Después de un mes.
   e. i. Eufórica

Chapter 2: Careers

Tu oficio es cotidiano y decisivo: mientras alumbre el sol, serás ardiente; mientras dure la vida, estarás vivo.

- Antonio Gala

Work tends to be a very important subject in everyone's life. That's why, in this second chapter, we will go deep into careers and jobs.

Vocabulary to talk about careers

	Estudié	en... hasta...
Soy Estoy	licenciada/o graduada/o diplomada/o	en...
Me	licencié gradué diplomé	en...

Tengo	experiencia	en... con... como...
	Aspiro	a...
Estoy	especializada/o	en...
Mis	logros	son... han sido...

Now, we'll see some of these expressions used in examples, for you to grasp their meaning:

- *Estudié en la Universidad de Madrid.* ("I studied at the University of Madrid.")
- *Soy diplomada en Lengua y Literatura.* ("I hold a diploma in Language and Literature.")
- *En 2015, me licencié en Literaturas Comparadas.* ("In 2015, I graduated in Comparative Literature.")
- *Tengo experiencia como docente de español.* ("I have experience as a Spanish teacher.")
- *Aspiro a ser investigadora.* ("I aspire to be a researcher.")
- *Estoy especializada en Literatura Peruana del siglo XX.* ("I'm specialized in 20th century Peruvian Literature.")

Vocabulary to talk about work

Now, let's see some questions for you to think about your own career, or to ask other people about theirs'.

- *¿Trabajas o has trabajado alguna vez?* ("Do you work, or have you ever worked?")
- *¿Has trabajado siempre en el mismo sector?* ("Have you always worked in the same sector")
- *Si cambiaste de sector, ¿por qué motivo fue?* ("If you have changed sectors, why was it?")
- *¿Qué te parece la idea de tener el mismo trabajo toda la vida?* ("What do you thing about the idea of having the same job all your life?")
- *¿Estarías dispuesto a trabajar en una industria que no tenga relación con tus estudios?* ("Would you be willing to work on an industry that's not related to your studies?")
- *¿En qué circunstancias lo harías?* ("Under which circumstances would you do it?")
- *¿Te parece una buena idea trabajar y estudiar a la vez?* ("Do you think that working and studying is a good idea?")

To answer these and other questions about jobs and career paths, you'll need some specific vocabulary, so let's take a look at it:

- **Matricularse en** + *la universidad, una carrera, un seminario, una clase* ("to enroll in + college, a degree, a seminar, a class")
- **Obtener** + *un título, una beca* ("to obtain + a degree, a scholarship")
- **Tener** + *un título, un grado, una beca, un máster, un doctorado* ("to have + a degree, a scholarship, a master's degree, a PhD")
- **Trabajar a** + *tiempo completo, tiempo parcial* ("to work + half time, full time")
- **Cambiar de** + *trabajo, empresa, sector, industria, puesto* ("to

change + jobs, companies, sectors, industries, positions")

- **Hacer** + *las prácticas, un curso de capacitación, una carrera* ("to do + an internship, a training course, a career")
- **Un trabajo** + *bien/mal remunerado/pago* ("a well-paid/badly-paid job")
- **Incorporarse a** + *un trabajo, una empresa* ("to join a job, a company")
- **Mercado** + *de trabajo, laboral* ("job market")
- **Dejar** + *un trabajo, los estudios* ("to leave + a job, college, university")
- **(Re)orientar** + *la carrera* ("to redirect + a career path")
- **Recibir** + *una indemnización, una orientación* ("to receive + an indemnification, a compensation")
- **Pasar de... a...** ("to go from... to...")
- **Reinventarse** ("to reinvent oneself")

Figurative language: verbs and expressions

In this section, we'll focus on some words and expressions in figurative language related to the work market.

- *En marketing, creemos que <u>acuñar</u> nuevos términos no es una buena estrategia de comunicación.* ("In marketing, we believe that coining new terms is not a good communication strategy.")

In its literal meaning, *acuñar una moneda* means making and putting into circulation a coin. There are other expressions that derive from this one: for example, *acuñar una palabra, acuñar un término*, and *acuñar una idea*. In these cases, it means giving form to an expression or concept, especially when it achieves diffusion or permanence.

- *Ya es hora de <u>darle una vuelta</u> a las formas de enseñar, ¿no crees?* ("It's high time we changed things a bit in education, don't you think?")

Tener una idea o un proyecto en la cabeza is having an idea or a project in your mind, but which is not yet completely clear: *hay que darle una vuelta*, i.e., you need to think about it more calmly, reflecting and looking for all the possibilities, with the intention of improving it.

- *Gracias a la contribución de todos los colaboradores, <u>ha florecido</u> una cultura empresarial muy beneficiosa.* ("Thanks to the contribution of all the collaborators, a very beneficial corporate culture has bloomed.")

When an idea or business goes well and thrives, we can use the verb *florecer* ("to flourish" or "to bloom"). In those cases, we are comparing the idea or business with a plant or tree.

- *En las horas tranquilas, para <u>matar el tiempo</u>, puedes organizar los archivos de la computadora.* ("In the quiet hours, to kill time, you can organize the files of the computer.")

In Spanish, the verb *matar* ("to kill") is commonly used in expressions such as *matar el hambre* ("to kill hunger"), and *matar el aburrimiento* ("to kill boredom"). In those cases, it means to make something stop being present. When we say *matar el tiempo* ("to kill time"), we mean getting busy with something to get the feeling that time is passing faster.

Collocations with *sacar* ("to take or bring up")

Collocations are words or other elements that commonly appear together and create a new meaning. Here are some examples.

- *Sacar partido* ("to benefit")
- *Sacar ventaja* ("to take advantage")
- *Sacar conclusiones* ("to draw conclusions")
- *Sacarle punta (a algo)* ("to sharpen")

- *Sacar un tema* ("to bring up a topic")
- *Sacar (el/los) boletos* ("to buy the tickets")
- *Sacar pecho* ("chest out means being brave and face a difficult situation")
- *Sacar el parecido* ("to guess the resemblance")
- *Sacar a colación* ("to mention")
- *Sacar adelante* ("to get something off the ground")

Now let's see these collocations in use:

- *Nos pidieron que sacáramos el proyecto adelante con la mitad de los fondos que nos habían prometido.* ("They asked us to get the project off the ground with half the funds they had promised.")
- *La situación es complicada, pero tienes que sacar pecho y seguir adelante. Tienes que sacarle partido a la adversidad.* ("It's a difficult situation, but you need to be brave and carry on. You have to take advantage of adversity.")
- *Me gustaría sacar a colación algunas de las cosas que se dijeron en la reunión.* ("I would like to bring up some of the issues mentioned during the meeting.")
- *Estuvieron debatiendo durante horas, pero no sacaron ninguna conclusión.* ("They debated for hours, but they didn't draw any conclusions.")

Verbal periphrasis to express beginning, development, progress, and ending

Spanish verbal periphrasis are expressions made up of at least two verbs: an auxiliary verb (which is conjugated) and a main verb (in the infinitive, gerund or participle). It's also common for a connector or linking word to be between them. They express a nuance or a change of modality of the main verb. Many verbal periphrasis are used to highlight in what stage an event is.

Beginning

comenzar a + infinitivo, empezar a + infinitivo, and *ponerse a + infinitivo*

We use these periphrasis to indicate the start of an action.

- *Comencé a estudiar español hace tres años.* ("I started studying Spanish three years ago.")
- *Empecé a tomar clases particulares el año pasado.* ("I started taking private lessons last year.")
- *Me puse a practicar conversación porque visitaré México pronto.* ("I started practicing conversation because I'm visiting Mexico soon.")

Ponerse a + infinitivo has two characteristics: on the one hand, it expresses a rapid onset, without transition; and on the other hand, it's usually combined with a subject who has control over the action.

- *Por la crisis, la compañía empezó a perder clientes.* ("Because of the crisis, the company started losing clients," but not *Por la crisis, la compañía se puso a perder clientes.*)

In addition to these periphrasis, there are other collocations expressing beginning but can only be combined with a limited number of infinitives:

- *Romper a + llorar, reír, gritar, aplaudir, llover*
- *Echarse a + llorar, reír, temblar*
- *Echar a + andar, caminar, correr, rodar*

Let's see some examples:

- *Cuando se enteró de la triste noticia, Román rompió a llorar.* (When he heard the sad news, Román burst into tears.")
- *Cuando entré a casa, vi que el perro había metido la cabeza en un bote de pintura y no pude más que echarme a reír.* ("When I entered my house, I saw the dog had put its head in a paint bucket, and I couldn't help bursting into laughter.")
- *Lautaro notó que Sofía se había olvidado las llaves y echó a correr detrás de ella para dárselas.* ("Lautaro realized Sofía had forgotten her keys, so he went running after her to give them back to her.")

Development

seguir + gerundio and *seguir + sin + infinitivo*

We use *seguir + gerundio* to express the continuity of an event.

- *Clara sigue trabajando en el restaurante de sus padres.* ("Clara is still working in her parents' restaurant.")

In its negative form, *seguir + sin + infinitivo*, it indicates that, against our expectations, an event hasn't been completed.

- *Clara sigue sin encontrar otro trabajo.* ("Clara still can't find another job;" she's been looking for a while, but she can't find one.")

ir + gerundio

We use this periphrasis to indicate that an event develops gradually, in different phases or stages, usually oriented towards a final result.

- *Le fue hablando de los cambios a medida que iban desarrollándose.* ("She told him about the changes while they

were happening.")
- Recupero *energía a medida que avanzo*. ("I recover energy as I go forward.")

In certain contexts, this periphrasis indicates the beginning of an action that develops gradually.

- *El examen es en dos semanas, vayan leyendo el material*. ("The exam is in two weeks; you should start reading the material.")
- *No me esperen, vayan comiendo*. ("Don't wait for me, start eating.")

venir + gerundio

We use this periphrasis to indicate that a process develops in phases from a previous moment, usually accompanied by a temporary complement that indicates the beginning or ending of the process.

- *Clara viene trabajando en el restaurante desde hace un tiempo*. ("Clara has been working at the restaurant for a while.")
- *¿Qué opinas de lo que vengo haciendo hasta ahora?* ("What do you think of what I've been doing so far?")
- *Viene pensando en el tema desde hace unas semanas* ("She's been thinking about the issue for a few weeks")

Its meaning is similar to the periphrasis *estar + gerundio*. However, *estar + gerundio* has a more general meaning: it doesn't imply that the process develops in phases from an earlier moment.

- *Clara está trabajando en el restaurante*. ("Clara is working at the restaurant." She's currently working there, we don't know since when.)
- *Está pensando en el tema desde hace una semana*. ("She's been

thinking about the issue for the last week." She's been thinking about it continuously.)

Interruption

dejar + de + infinitivo

This periphrasis is used to indicate that an event has been interrupted.

- *Clara ha dejado de trabajar en el restaurante de sus padres.* ("Clara has stopped working in her parents' restaurant." She no longer works in the restaurant.)

Unlike *terminar + de + infinitivo*, we use *dejar + de + infinitivo* when we want to emphasize that the event has not reached its intended end but has been interrupted before reaching its end.

- *Los obreros terminaron de trabajar.* ("The laborers finished working.")
- *Los obreros dejaron de trabajar* ("The laborers stopped working.")
- *La mesa 15 ha terminado de comer* ("Table 15 has finished eating." There's no food left.)
- *La mesa 15 ha dejado de comer* ("Table 15 has stopped eating." There's food but they are no longer eating it.)

Dejar + de + infinitivo is especially used to express the interruption of a habit:

- *¿Has dejado de fumar?* ("Have you quit smoking?")
- *He dejado de trabajar en el restaurante de mis padres.* ("I've stopped working in my parents' restaurant.")

In its negative form, *no dejar + de + infinitivo*, it expresses that an event continues despite contrary expectations.

- *Clara no ha dejado de trabajar en el restaurante.* ("Clara has not stopped working in the restaurant." She continues working there, even if someone may think otherwise.)

Ending

terminar + gerundio

We use this periphrasis to place an action at the end of a series of actions or events.

- *Después de años en el restaurante de sus padres, Clara terminó trabajando en el lugar donde quería.* ("After years working at her parent's restaurant, Clara ended up working at the place she wanted.")

It usually implies a positive or negative evaluation of the entire sequence of actions.

- *Clara tuvo mala suerte. Le iba muy bien en la universidad, pero le costó mucho conseguir trabajo y terminó trabajando en el restaurante de sus padres, que no era lo que quería.* ("Clara was unlucky. She was successful at school, but she had trouble getting a job, so she ended up working in her parents' restaurant, which wasn't what she wanted.")

It is important to distinguish it from *terminar + de + infinitivo*, which expresses that an event has been completed.

- *Terminé de limpiar la casa.* ("I've finished cleaning the house.")
- *Terminé limpiando la casa.* ("I ended up cleaning the house," even though it wasn't on my plans.)

Resources to make a comparison

Read these phrases about the state of education in Spain where comparisons are made.

- *Los ingresos todavía son muy superiores para aquellos que tienen estudios universitarios, o incluso terciarios, <u>con respecto a</u> los que se quedaron solo con el instituto.* ("Income is still much higher for those who have a university degree, or even a tertiary degree, compared to those who stopped studying after high school.")
- *En España, se invierte un 7% del PBI en educación, <u>mientras que</u> la media de la OCDE es solo del 3%.* ("In Spain, 7% of GDP is invested in education, while the OECD average is only 7%.")

These are see some more expressions with similar meanings that can be used to make comparisons:

- *Aunque:* although
- *Comparado con:* compared to, with
- *En cambio:* whereas
- *En comparación con:* in comparison with

Mientras, mientras que

In the second example sentence from above, *mientras* is used to make a comparison, but it can also be used to express simultaneity. However, the word is not used exactly in the same way for both cases. Look at the examples and try to identify how it is used in each case.

- *Mientras yo pongo la mesa, tú puedes terminar de hacer la cena.* ("While I set the table, you can finish making dinner.")
- *Mientras que yo pongo la mesa, tú puedes terminar de hacer la*

~~cena.~~

- *A Manolo le gustan las matemáticas, mientras que Marco prefiere la historia.* ("Manolo likes math, while Marcos prefers history")
- *A Manolo le gustan las matemáticas, mientras Marco prefiere la historia.*

To compare two elements, you can use *mientras* and *mientras que*, although *mientras que* is preferable. To talk about two simultaneous actions in time, only *mientras* is correct.

Antes que, antes de

To express a preference when comparing two elements, it's common to use *antes*. Take a look at these examples and try to guess the usage rules.

- *Antes que verlo arruinado, prefiero prestarle dinero.* ("Before seen him ruined, I'd rather lend him money")
- ~~*Antes de verlo arruinado, prefiero prestarle dinero.*~~
- *Antes de terminar, quiero preguntarte algo importante.* ("Before we finish, I want to ask you something important")
- ~~*Antes que terminar, quiero preguntarte algo importante.*~~

To indicate that something is preferred over something else, we use *antes que*. To indicate that something is previous in time, we use *antes de*.

Más de, menos de, más que, menos que

Next, we'll read some examples with quantities and comparisons. Pay attention to the uses of *más de*, *menos de*, *más que*, and *menos que*. Below, there's a chart with the usage rules.

- *En España se invierte más en educación que en la media de los países de la OCDE, hay más horas de enseñanza y el ratio profesor-alumno es menor que en otros países.* ("In Spain there is more investment in education than in the average OECD countries, there are more teaching hours, and the teacher-student ratio is lower than in other countries.")
- *En España, más de un 20% de los jóvenes que no tienen estudios superiores están desempleados.* ("In Spain, more than 20% of young people without higher education are unemployed.")
- *Para solucionar el problema, necesitamos más que palabras, hay que actuar.* ("To solve the problem, we need more than words, we have to act.")
- *Existe una diferencia salarial importante entre hombres y mujeres: en puestos similares, las mujeres tienden a ganar menos que los hombres.* ("There is an important pay gap between men and women: in similar positions, women tend to earn less than men.")
- *El salario mínimo en España es algo más de setecientos euros al mes.* ("The minimum wage in Spain is just over seven hundred euros per month.")
- *La crisis ha hecho más que aumentar el desempleo: ha destrozado la vida de muchas personas.* ("The crisis has done more than increase unemployment: it has shattered the lives of many.")

	Más/menos de	Más/menos que
To compare two elements		x
To mention a	x	

quantity without comparing it with another		
To correct a piece of information, adding a new idea		x

No + verbo + más que/de

The expression *no + verbo + más que* can be used in the sense of *solamente* (only):

- *En su nuevo cargo, Luca no gana más que mil euros al mes. Con eso no puede mantener su estilo de vida...* ("In his new position, Luca earns no more than a thousand euros a month. That's not enough to keep up with his lifestyle..." Luca earns only a thousand euros a month.)
- *No sé cuánto gana Luca, pero no es más de mil euros al mes.* ("I don't know how much Luca makes, but it's not more than a thousand euros a month.")

Cuanto más/menos..., más/menos...

We use these constructions to express that the variation (increase or decrease) of something entails a variation of something else.

- *Cuanto más lee, menos entiende.* ("The more she reads, the less she understands.")
- *Cuanto más grande soy, más me parezco a mi hermano.* ("The older I am, the more I looks like my brother.")

When modifying a noun, the quantifier *cuanto* has to agree in gender and number with it. When it's used together with an adjective or an adverb, it remains invariable.

- *Cuanta más fruta comes, mejor te sientes.* ("The more fruit you eat, the better you feel.")
- *Cuanto más guapos son, más vanidosos.* ("The more handsome they are, the more vain they are.")
- *Cuanto más cerca vive, más tarde llega* ("The closer he lives, the later he arrives.")

The sentences with *cuanto* are usually constructed in the present or imperfect past of the indicative (to express present or past habits), or in the present subjunctive (to express possible future events).

- *Cuanto más estudio, mejor me va.* ("The more I study, the better I do.")
- *Cuanto más estudiaba, mejor me iba.* ("The more I studied, the better I did.")
- *Cuanto más estudie, mejor me irá.* ("The more I study, the better I'll do.")

Exercises

1. Fill in the gaps with a word from the box

experiencia - licenciada - especializada - gradué

    a. Me llamo Sofía. Soy .... en Comunicación Social.

    b. Me .... en el 2010.

    c. Tengo .... como periodista.

    d. Estoy .... en periodismo audiovisual.

2. Match the question with the possible answers

    a. ¿Has trabajado siempre en el mismo sector?

    b. ¿Por qué motivo cambiaste de sector?

    c. ¿Te parece una buena idea trabajar y estudiar a la vez?

    d. ¿Qué te parece la idea de tener un mismo empleo toda la vida?

        i.   Creo que me aburriría. Me gusta mucho el cambio.

        ii.   No, he cambiado varias veces.

        iii.   La mayoría de las veces porque me ofrecían más dinero en otro sector.

        iv.   No, me parece mejor enfocarse en una sola cosa.

3. Decide whether the following statements are true or false. Correct the false ones

    a. En un sentido literal, "acuñar" significa darle forma a ideas o conceptos.

    b. "Darle la vuelta a una idea" es pensar en un asunto con más claridad.

    c. "Florecer" se usa con el sentido de fracasar.

d. "Matar el tiempo" se usa como sinónimo de hacer algo para distraerse.

4. Fill in the gaps with one of the collocations of the verb "sacar" that we saw on this chapter
   a. Me suena su cara, pero no le saco ....
   b. Quiero aprovechar la ocasión para sacar .... algo que quería mencionarte.
   c. Se apresuraron a sacar .... y lo despidieron sin tener pruebas.
   d. ¿Ya has sacado .... de avión para tus vacaciones?

5. Decide which of the following expressions could replace the bolded words in the sentences below

   ┌──┐
   │ no se habían investigado - se investiga - todavía no se investiga lo │
   │   suficiente   │
   └──┘

   a. Desde que en 2004 se acuñara el término e-learning, **no se ha dejado de investigar** sobre las maneras de aprender de manera virtual.
   b. Diez años después, los problemas fundamentales **seguían sin investigarse**.
   c. El problema es que **se sigue investigando muy poco** al respecto.

6. Choose the correct verbal periphrasis to express beginning to complete the sentences
   a. .... expresa un comienzo abrupto, sin transición.
   b. .... suele combinarse con un sujeto agente.

c. .... , ... y .... indican
   el inicio de una acción.

d. ...., ... y .... se usan
   con verbos como *llorar, reír, gritar, andar, correr*, etc.
   para indicar comienzo.

7. Choose the correct verbal periphrasis to express development to
   complete the sentences
   a. .... se usa para expresar la continuidad de un
      evento.
   b. .... indica que un evento que se esperaba que
      sucediera, no ha tenido lugar.
   c. Usamos .... para indicar que un evento se
      desarrolla de forma gradual.
   d. .... indica que un proceso se está
      desarrollando en fases desde un momento anterior.

8. Choose the correct verbal periphrasis to express interruption to
   complete the sentences.
   a. .... indica que se interrumpió un evento.
   b. .... se usa cuando la acción alcanzó el objetivo
      planeado.
   c. .... se usa para expresar la interrupción de un
      hábito.
   d. La forma .... expresa que un evento continúa
      a pesar de que se esperaba lo contrario.
   e. .... pone a una acción al final de una serie de
      eventos.

9. Fill in the gaps with *mientras* or *mientras que*
   a. .... tú terminas de arreglarte voy a ir pidiendo
      un taxi.

b. Martha toma clases los lunes, ... Susana lo hace los jueves.

c. El equipo de marketing presentó el informe en nueve meses, ... que de contabilidad tardó veintiséis.

d. Aprovechó para bañarse .... se calentaba la comida.

10. Fill in the gaps with *cuanto, cuantos, cuanta,* or *cuantas.*

a. .... más lejos quieras ir, más caro va a ser el pasaje.

b. .... más flores cortes, pero se verá el jardín.

c. .... menos gaseosa bebas, menos caries tendrás.

Answer Key

1.
   a. licenciada
   b. gradué
   d. experiencia
   e. especializada

2. .
   a. ii.
   b. iii.
   c. iv.
   d. i.

3.
   a. False. En su sentido metafórico, "acuñar" significa darle forma a ideas o conceptos.
   b. True.
   c. False. "Florecer" se usa con el sentido de prosperar y crecer en riqueza o reputación.
   d. True.

4.
   a. el parecido
   b. a colación
   c. conclusiones
   d. los boletos

5.
   a. se investiga
   b. no se habían investigado
   c. todavía no se investiga lo suficiente

6.
   a. Ponerse a + infinitivo
   b. Ponerse a + infinitivo

    c. Comenzar a + infinitivo; empezar a + infinitivo; ponerse a + infinitivo

    d. Romper a; echarse a; echar a

7. .

    a. Seguir + gerundio

    b. Seguir + sin + infinitivo

    c. ir + gerundio

    d. Venir + gerundio

8. .

    a. Dejar + de + infinitivo

    b. Terminar + de + infinitivo

    c. Dejar + de + infinitivo

    d. no dejar + de + infinitivo

    e. Terminar + gerundio

9.

    a. mientras

    b. mientras que

    c. mientras que

    d. mientras

10.

    a. cuanto

    b. cuantas

    c. cuanta

Chapter 3: Anecdotes and Gossip

Tus manos, heridas de intrincados caminos, son la historia de una raza de amadores.

- Alfonsina Storni

Welcome to chapter 3! In this chapter, we will learn to narrate interesting anecdotes like a native. We will also learn many resources to gossip wherever you go. Are you ready?

Direct and Indirect Speech

There are two main ways to replicate someone's speech: through direct or indirect speech. Let's have a look at both of them!

Saying Verbs

We can't always resort to the good old *decir*. In Spanish, repeating words isn't common, and it's actually a bit annoying to the reader, so we usually use different verbs. Of course, when it comes to oral speech, we most likely will say *decir* all the time, but at this level we're past learning the easiest ways, right?

Let's have a look at some important and usual verbs of saying!

- *Afirmar*: to claim, to assert
- *Exclamar*: to exclaim
- *Preguntar*: to ask (a question)

- *Pedir*: to ask (for something)
- *Negar*: to negate
- *Ordenar*: to order
- *Recordar*: to remind
- *Aclarar*: to clear, clarify
- *Repetir*: to repeat
- *Asegurar*: to ensure
- *Sugerir*: to suggest
- *Comentar*: to comment
- *Precisar*: to specify
- *Contar*: to tell
- *Proponer*: to propose
- *Explicar*: to explain

Adverbs Ending in *-mente*

With the saying verbs, we might sometimes want to add some adverbs ending in -*mente* so that we can say how someone said what they said. For example, we can say: *aclaró rápidamente, repitió insistentemente*, or *habló lentamente*.

Adverbs ending in -*mente* are formed with the feminine singular form of adjectives and the ending -*mente*. Let's see a few adjectives and how to turn them into adverbs that you can use to describe the way people speak!

- *rápido → rápidamente* ("quickly")
- *lento → lentamente* ("slowly")
- *continuo → continuamente* ("continuously")
- *feliz → felizmente* ("happily")
- *efusivo → efusivamente* ("effusively")
- *rotundo → rotundamente* ("roundly or emphatically")
- *enfático → enfáticamente* ("emphatically")

And there is one more way in which we can use adverbs ending in -*mente* when we're telling anecdotes: to express our assessment of the situation. When we use adverbs ending in -*mente* in this way, we separate it from the rest of the sentence by a short pause or commas when we're writing, and we can place it at the beginning, in the middle or at the end of the sentence. Let's have a look at a few adverbs we can use when we're telling anecdotes!

- *lógicamente* ("logically")
  - *Lógicamente, me fui de ahí tan rápido como pude.* ("logically, I got out of there as fast as I could.")
- *desgraciadamente* ("unfortunately")
  - *No encontré la bebida que me pediste, desgraciadamente.* ("I couldn't find the beverage you asked, unfortunately.")
- *desafortunadamente* ("unfortunately")
  - *Lo intenté, pero, desafortunadamente, no pude lograrlo.* ("I tried, but, unfortunately, I couldn't do it.")
- *afortunadamente* ("fortunately")
  - *Afortunadamente, logré hacer todo a tiempo.* ("Fortunately, I could do everything in time.")
- *paradójicamente* ("paradoxically")
  - *Paradójicamente, Laura aprendió a bailar tango en Japón.* ("Paradoxically, Laura learned to dance tango in Japan.")
- *curiosamente* ("curiously")
  - *Pablo va todos los años a la misma playa, curiosamente.* ("Pablo goes to the same beach every year, curiously.")

Direct Speech

Direct speech is probably the easiest way of reproducing someone else's speech. To use it, we simply need to use a verb of saying followed by a colon and inverted commas. We put what the person said between the inverted commas, and we don't modify it at all. Let's see some examples:

- *Paola afirmó rotundamente: "Nadie entrará en esta habitación".* ("Paola asserted emphatically: "Nobody will enter this room.")
- *Facundo me dijo: "No quiero verte más".* ("Facundo told me: "I don't want to see you anymore.")
- *Ayer hablé con Mariana y me preguntó: "¿Dónde te haces las uñas?"* ("Yesterday I talked to Mariana and she asked me: 'Where do you get your nails done?'")

This way of reproducing other people's speech is used to make anecdotes more intense, dramatic, natural, lively and expressive! It is also the preferred way of reproducing speech in formal speeches, essays and written texts.

In some cases, we might want to say who did the person say what we're quoting to. As we can see from the third sentence, if they said it to me, we simply add *me* before the verb of saying. However, if it is somebody else, we need to add the indirect object pronoun before the verb of saying followed by *a* + the name of the person, just like with any other indirect object. If we're already talking about the interlocutor, we don't need to add the name, of course, only the indirect object pronoun that refers to them. J

Let's see a few examples:

- *Facundo le dijo a Anabel: "No quiero verte más".* ("Facundo told Anabel: "I don't want to see you anymore.")
- *Lucas y María hablaron con Francisco y les preguntó: "¿Qué computadora usan?"* ("Yesterday, Lucas and María talked to Francisco and he asked them: "What computer do you use?")

Indirect Speech

Indirect speech also requires the use of a saying verb, but this time we don't need to add a colon or inverted commas. In this case, we add *que* after the saying verb and then we reproduce the speech. However, we don't reproduce the speech exactly, we need to interpret it and modify it. Just like in English, we need to modify verb tenses and deictic words and phrases. Let's first see how this looks, and then we'll break it all down.

- *Paola afirmó rotundamente que nadie entraría en esa habitación.* ("Paola asserted strongly that nobody would enter that room.")
- *Facundo dijo que no quería verlo más.* ("Facundo said that he didn't want to see him anymore.")
- *Ayer hablé con Mariana y me preguntó dónde me hacía las uñas.* ("Yesterday I talked to Mariana, and she asked me where I got my nails done.")

As we've seen, after the verb of saying we need to add *que,* which introduces the subordinate clause that contains someone's message. But if the message is a subordinate clause, it needs to be like any other sentence and, therefore, it should at least have a subject (which may or may not be overt) and a verb.

However, as you might have noticed in the third example, after *preguntar* we never say *que*. Instead, we use *si* for yes/no questions, and the interrogative adverb for wh- questions. That's why in the example we have *me preguntó dónde me hacía las uñas,* and we could have never had *me preguntó que me hacía las uñas.*

It's time to talk about the hard part of indirect speech: deictic words and expressions, and verbs. Deictic words and expressions are those that refer to the time, place or situation the speaker is in when they are talking. The words and phrases that need to change are adverbs, pronouns, and determinants. Some clear examples of deictics in English are "today," "this," "now," etc., which means that their Spanish equivalents (*hoy, esto, ahora,* etc.) are also deictics. Unless we are in the same communicative setting as when the speaker said what we are reproducing, then we can't use *hoy, esto,* or *ahora* like we would in direct speech.

Let's see some examples of this in which we compare direct and indirect speech:

- *Carolina dijo: "Hoy no quiero cenar".* ("Carolina said: 'I don't want to have dinner today.'")
  - *Carolina dijo que ese día no quería cenar.* ("Carolina said that she didn't want to have dinner that day.")
- *Cuando estábamos en la playa, Gerardo exclamó: "¡No quiero irme de aquí!"* ("When we were at the beach, Gerardo exclaimed: 'I don't want to leave this place!'")
  - *Cuando estábamos en la playa, Gerardo exclamó que no quería irse de allí.* ("When we were at the beach, Gerardo exclaimed that he didn't want to leave that place.")

Of course, in the first example, if we're replicating what Carolina said later the same day, we could still say *hoy,* and if we're saying it the day after, we could change the deictic word for *ayer.*

As we mentioned, other important deictic parts of speech are pronouns! We can't say ~~Carolina dijo que hoy yo no quiero comer~~ because that would mean an absolutely different thing! Of course, in Spanish the pronouns aren't always overt and we usually know the person and number of the subject based on the verbs, which is one of the reasons we also need to change verbs!

In Spanish verbs do not only change in indirect speech because of the person and number, they also need to change because we are talking about something that happened before. In English, this happens with indirect speech too, and we need to, for example, change the present simple tense for the simple past tense. Luckily, we have a table that will help you see how to change the tenses in Spanish with some examples!

Direct speech	→	Indirect speech
Presente de indicativo *Ella dijo: "No <u>como</u> arroz".*	→	Pretérito imperfecto de indicativo *Ella dijo que no <u>comía</u> arroz.*
Pretérito perfecto compuesto *Ella dijo: "No <u>he comido</u> arroz en años".*	→	Pretérito pluscuamperfecto *Ella dijo que no <u>había comido</u> arroz en años.*
Pretérito imperfecto de indicativo *Ella dijo: "No <u>comía</u> arroz cuando era pequeña".*	→	Pretérito imperfecto de indicativo *Ella dijo que no <u>comía</u> arroz cuando era pequeña.*
Pretérito perfecto simple *Ella dijo: "No <u>comí</u> arroz ayer".*	→	Pretérito pluscuamperfecto *Ella dijo que no había comido arroz el día anterior.*
Pretérito pluscuamperfecto *Ella dijo: "No <u>había comido</u> arroz en años".*	→	Pretérito pluscuamperfecto *Ella dijo que no <u>había comido</u> arroz en años.*
Futuro *Ella dijo: "No <u>comeré</u> arroz".*	→	Condicional simple *Ella dijo que no <u>comería</u> arroz.*
Condicional simple *Ella dijo: "No <u>comería</u> arroz si*	→	Condicional simple *Ella dijo que no <u>comería</u>*

no me obligaran".		*arroz si no la obligaran.*
Presente de subjuntivo *Ella dijo: "No quiero que* <u>*comas*</u> *arroz".*	→	Pretérito imperfecto de subjuntivo *Ella dijo que no quería que yo* <u>*comiera*</u> *arroz.*
Pretérito imperfecto de subjuntivo *Ella dijo: "No quería que* <u>*comieras*</u> *arroz"*	→	Pretérito imperfecto de subjuntivo *Ella dijo que no quería que yo* <u>*comiera*</u> *arroz.*
Imperativo *Ella dijo: "No* <u>*comas*</u> *arroz,* <u>*come*</u> *ensalada"*	→	Pretérito imperfecto de subjuntivo *Ella me dijo que no* <u>*comiera*</u> *arroz, que* <u>*comiera*</u> *ensalada.*

You may be wondering why we would choose to go through all this trouble to use indirect speech when we have direct speech. Actually, indirect speech is preferred in oral contexts and when we want to make a comment or express our perception of what someone else said. When we use the third-person, it can also give a sense of depersonalization and abstraction.

Before we finish this section, we should mention that there are some verbs that we can use in indirect speech that summarize the words of part of a conversation so that you don't have to add *que* and what the other person said. One example of this in English would be the verb "to thank." Instead of saying "He said 'Thank you'" or "He told me he thanked me," we could simply say "He thanked me." And the same happens in Spanish with the following verbs:

- *Agradecer* ("to thank")

- *Lila me agradeció por el regalo.* ("Lila thanked me for the present.")
- *Dar las gracias* ("to thank")
  - *Lila me dio las gracias por el regalo.* ("Lila thanked me for the present.")
- *Disculparse* ("to say sorry")
  - *Lila se disculpó por su comportamiento.* ("Lila said she was sorry for her behavior.")
- *Quejarse* ("to complain")
  - *Lila se quejó de su maestra.* ("Lila complained about her teacher.")
- *Saludar* ("to greet")
  - *Lila me saludó ayer en la calle.* ("Lila greeted me in the street yesterday.")
- *Despedirse* ("to say goodbye")
  - *Lila se despidió con un discurso.* ("Lila said goodbye with a speech.")
- *Felicitar* ("to congratulate")
  - *Lila me felicitó por mi trabajo.* ("Lila congratulated me for my work.")

Relative Constructions with *lo*

Another resource especially useful when we are gossiping is to use the relative constructions with *lo de* and *lo que*. We use these structures to refer to a topic that is or may be known to the people in the conversation. Let's see a few examples first:

- *¿Has oído lo de Catalina?* ("Have you heard what happened to Catalina?")

- *No, ¿qué?* ("No, what?")

- *Pues que ha tenido un accidente.* ("Well, she has had an accident")

○ *¡No lo puedo creer!* ("I can't believe it!")

- *Ayer Francisco contó <u>lo que</u> le pasó a Catalina.* ("Yesterday Francisco told what happened to Catalina")

○ *Sí, me he enterado. Es terrible, pero me alegra que esté bien.* ("Yes, I've heard. It's awful, but I'm glad she's fine")

- *<u>Lo de</u> tener un accidente así me parece horrible.* ("Having such an accident seems horrible to me")

As you can see from these examples, we can use *lo de* with both nouns and verbs in the infinitive, but we can only use *lo que* with conjugated verbs.

There is one more way in which we can refer to different situations and anecdotes which is by mixing the two we've seen before. We can use *lo de que* with whole sentences in the indicative or subjunctive. Let's see some examples.

- *¿Es cierto <u>lo de que</u> Mónica se va a vivir a Italia?* (Is it true that Mónica is going to live in Italy?")

○ *¡Sí, es cierto!* ("Yes, it's true!")

- *<u>Lo de que</u> comas más verduras me parece una buena idea.* ("That you eat more vegetables seems like a good idea")

○ *¡Gracias, a mí también!* ("Thanks, I think so too!")

Asserting and Hedging

To assert what we're saying, we can add some set phrases like *sin ninguna duda, sin duda, con toda seguridad,* and *con toda probabilidad.* For example, we can say "*Sin ninguna duda, mañana lloverá*" ("Without a doubt, it will rain tomorrow"). Another way to reinforce the truth or validity of our statement would be to use the present indicative.

In contrast, to attenuate what we're saying and hedge it, we can use phrases like *al parecer, de alguna manera, en cierto sentido,* and *según parece.* One example could be "*En cierto sentido, creo que este auto es mejor que el anterior*" ("In a sense, I think this car is better than the previous one"). In this sentence, we're not asserting that we think that, but we're establishing beforehand that we might not be completely certain. Finally, another resource we can use to hedge is using the simple conditional tense, which will allow us to express that what we're saying is a supposition, a hypothesis or something we heard. For example, we can say: "*El comportamiento de Bruno reflejaría que está pasando por un momento difícil*" ("Bruno's behavior would reflect that he's going through a tough time").

It's time to see an example conversation with everything we've seen so far!

- ¿Has oído lo que ocurrió ayer?

○ ¡No, cuéntamelo!

- ¡Parece que Miguel y Belén se van a casar!

○ ¿En serio? ¡No puedo creerlo! ¿Cómo fue?

- Bueno, estábamos almorzando y él se arrodilló en frente de todos y le preguntó si quería casarse con él. Ella lloró y ¡dijo que sí!

○ ¡Qué romántico! Lo de que todo el mundo se case ahora me da un poco de celos. ¡Yo también quiero algo así!

● Bueno, sin ninguna duda eso te sucederá a ti también. No te preocupes.

○ Gracias. ¿Y qué más sucedió?

● Bueno, al parecer no pierden el tiempo y ya empezaron a planearlo todo. El casamiento sería en diciembre.

○ ¡Qué lindo!

Consecutive Conjunctions and Connectors

To express consequence we can use conjunction or connectors. Consecutive conjunctions introduce subordinate sentences, occupy the first position in the sentence they introduce, and are separated from the main sentence by a comma or semicolon. These are some consecutive conjunctions:

- *de modo que*: "so"
  - *No estaba de buen humor, de modo que vi una película y me quedé en casa.* ("I wasn't in a good mood, so I saw a movie and stayed at home.")
- *por lo que*: "so"
  - *No tenía hambre, por lo que no comí.* ("I wasn't hungry, so I didn't eat.")
- *así que*: "so"
  - *Tenía frío, así que me puse una chaqueta.* ("I was cold, so I put on a jacket.")
- *de ahí (que)*: "hence," "which is why." This one in particular should be followed by a subjunctive because the consequence is a known fact that can be constructed as a sentence (preceded by *que*) or as a noun (without *que*).
  - *Estaba enferma, de ahí que faltara a clase.* ("I was sick, which is why I didn't go to class.")

- *Estaba enferma, <u>de ahí</u> <u>mi ausencia</u>.* ("I was sick, hence my absence.")

On the other hand, we have consecutive connectors which can be placed at the beginning, in the middle or at the end of the sentence and is separated from the rest of the elements by a pause in oral speech or a comma in written speech. Moreover, they can affect the whole sentence or only a part of it. Let's see a few of these connectors with some examples.

- *por ello/eso*: "which is why," "for that reason"
  - *Mis gatos son muy traviesos. <u>Por eso</u>, les compro juguetes para que no rompan mis cosas.* ("My cats are very playful. For that reason I buy them toys so they don't break my things.")
- *por (lo) tanto*: "therefore"
  - *Mi hermana tiene cinco años, está interesada en la música, <u>por lo tanto</u>, está aprendiendo a tocar violín.* ("My sister is five, she is interested in music, therefore, she is learning to play the violin.")
- *por consiguiente*: "consequently"
  - *Me enfermé y, <u>por consiguiente</u>, mi hermano se contagió.* ("I was sick and, consequently, my brother got infected too.")
- *en consecuencia*: "in consequence"
  - *Estaba muy ocupado y olvidé ir a buscar a mi hijo al colegio, <u>en consecuencia</u>.* ("I was really busy and I forgot to pick up my son from school, in consequence.")
- *Por consiguiente:* "consequently"
  - *A Leonardo le ofrecieron un mejor puesto de trabajo en Lisboa que le hará ganar más experiencia, más conocimiento y, por consiguiente, mucho más dinero en*

el futuro. ("Leonardo was offered a better job position in Lisbon that will make him earn more experience, more knowledge and, consequently, much more money in the future.")

- *así pues*: "therefore"
  - *Con mis ingresos ya no podía mantener el auto, <u>así pues</u>, lo vendí.* ("With my income I could no longer keep my car, therefore, I sold it.")
- *pues*: "thus". This connector can express cause and consequence depending on its position. When it is at the beginning of the sentence that introduces, it expresses cause, but when it is in the middle or at the end of the sentence, it expresses consequence.
  - *No pudo venir a clase, <u>pues</u> su padre estaba enfermo.* ("He couldn't come to class because his father was sick") → cause
  - *Su padre estaba enfermo, no pudo, <u>pues</u>, venir a clase.* ("His father was sick, he couldn't, thus, come to class") → consequence

Exercises

1. Here are five things that Flavio said to different people yesterday. Can you turn them into direct speech?
    a. A Lucía: Creo que necesitas descansar, te veo muy estresada.
    b. A Pedro: Cuando yo era pequeño, no me gustaba jugar a las escondidas.
    c. A Norma: Si quieres conseguir algo, debes luchar por eso.
    d. A Lidia: Mañana iré a pescar con mi suegro, esperamos que esté soleado.
    e. A Santiago: ¿Quieres venir a mi casa a cenar mañana?

2. Here are five things that Milagros said to different people yesterday. Can you turn the direct speech versions into indirect speech?
    a. Milagros rápidamente le aseguró a Gonzalo: "Todo irá bien".
    b. Milagros le contó efusivamente a Daniela: "Mariana y Darío están saliendo".
    c. Milagros le preguntó a Fabiana enfáticamente: "¿A qué hora quieres salir mañana?"
    d. Milagros le comentó a Bruno: "Desgraciadamente debo trabajar mañana"
    e. Milagros le pidió a Clara: "¿Puedes prestarme un lápiz?"

3. Fill in the gaps with *lo de, lo que* or *lo de que* where appropriate.
    a. .... no se pueda estacionar en la plaza me parece un disparate.
    b. ¿Puedes creer .... me dijo Patricio ayer?
    c. Me parece un poco extraño .... Samanta, ¿y a ti?

d. .... escuché ayer en tu casa no me hizo gracia.

e. ¿....................... cantar y bailar en la fiesta del sábado es solo para los niños?

4. Miranda is gossiping with Diego about what Nancy did last weekend, but she's heard it from Gabriel, so she isn't sure about the facts. Choose the right phrase or word in each sentence so that Miranda's speech doesn't seem like she's certain about what she's saying.

   a. Parece/Sin duda que Miranda fue a una fiesta el sábado y se cayó.

   b. No solo eso, sino que con toda seguridad/al parecer se manchó el vestido y tuvo que irse.

   c. De alguna manera/Con toda probabilidad, se encontró con su padre que no sabía que ella había ido a una fiesta.

   d. Sin ninguna duda/Al parecer su padre la regañó y está castigada.

5. Complete the following sentences with phrases from the box.

¿entiendes? - y eso - ¿y qué pasó? - pura - ¿todavía no entregaste la tarea?

---

   a. Juan, ... Era para la semana pasada. ¿Qué estuviste haciendo?

   b. Creo que todo en esta vida es .... suerte. Aunque hagas todo bien, todo puede salir mal.

   c. Mañana iré a tu casa antes de tu cumpleaños para ayudarte a preparar la comida, poner los platos ...., ¿te parece?

   d. Quiero irme de viaje, pero ahora no puedo gastar dinero en eso, ...

e. Le dije que no tenía que jugar con el florero porque se rompería .... Se rompió, por supuesto.

6. Look at the following questions and statements and choose the answer that expresses doubt.
   a. Cuando llegué, no había nadie en casa.
      i. ¿Cuándo?
      ii. ¿No había nadie en casa?
      iii. ¿Llegaste?
   b. Fuimos a una fiesta de cumpleaños esa noche... ¿de quién era?
      i. ¿De Juan?
      ii. ¿Juan fue a la fiesta?
      iii. ¿A dónde crees que vas?
   c. Luego Felicia salió a buscarme y también se perdió.
      i. ¿Tú te perdiste?
      ii. ¿Quién?
      iii. ¿Felicia salió?

7. Look at the following questions and statements and choose the answer that expresses surprise.
   a. Parece que cuando Bruno se desmayó nadie supo qué hacer.
      i. ¿No había nadie?
      ii. Bruno no se desmayó.
      iii. ¡Pero si son todos médicos!
   b. Después de que Graciela se cayera, todos nos reímos.
      i. Pero Graciela no se cayó.
      ii. ¿Graciela se cayó?
      iii. Yo no me reí.
   c. Al final, Nicolás y Tomás se pelearon.
      i. ¡Pero si siempre fueron mejores amigos!

ii. No me parece que se hayan peleado
iii. ¿Pedro y Juan se pelearon?

8. Read the following anecdote and then read what Gloria said when she told the anecdote to her daughter later that day. Can you correct her statements as if you were next to her at the time she told them?

Cecilia tuvo el peor día de su vida. El despertador no sonó esta mañana, así que se quedó dormida. Cuando se levantó, eran las 10 de la mañana y ella tenía que entrar a trabajar a las 9. No tuvo tiempo de bañarse ni desayunar, así que se cambió y salió corriendo. Tomó un taxi para no llegar más tarde, pero había mucho tráfico. Llegó a la oficina a las 11 y su jefe la regañó.

    a. Parece que cuando Cecilia se levantó, ya eran las 11 de la mañana.
    b. Antes de salir, se bañó y desayunó.
    c. Fue en bicicleta al trabajo.
    d. Llegó tarde y su secretaria la regañó.

9. Complete the following sentences with a consecutive conjunction or connector from the box below.

> *por ello - así que - pues - de ahí que*

    a. Me dolió la panza todo el día, ... no comiera.
    b. Me gusta muchísimo comprar libros. .... tengo una biblioteca tan grande.
    c. El auto de Beatriz está averiado, no puede, ..., recorrer grandes distancias hasta que lo arregle.
    d. Hugo no quería llevar al perro, ... lo llevé yo.

10. Read the following conversation between Marcela (•) and Jimena (○) and answer the questions in Spanish below.

• Parece que Jazmín tiene un novio nuevo. Los vi juntos el otro día en un café, pero ellos no me vieron. Mientras esperaba mi comida, escuché que él le recordaba a ella que su aniversario era el fin de semana siguiente y ella se quedó perpleja, ¿sabes?

○ ¿Se quedó perpleja? ¿Crees que es porque ella no quiere estar con él?

• No lo sé, pero ella se quedó sin palabras. Después de eso ella casi no habló y él le preguntó si ocurría algo, pero ella dijo que todo estaba bien.

○ ¡Qué extraño!

   a. ¿Dónde vio Marcela a Jazmín?

   b. ¿Qué le recordó el novio a Jazmín?

   c. Cuál fue la intención de Jimena cuando contestó "¿Se quedó perpleja?"

      i. Expresar duda sobre lo que dijo Marcela

      ii. Expresar sorpresa

   d. ¿Qué le preguntó el novio a Jazmín? ¿Podrías escribirlo en discurso directo?

Answer Key

1.

   a. Flavio/él le dijo/afirmó/sugirió a Lucía: "Creo que necesitas descansar, te veo muy estresada".

   b. Flavio/él le dijo/afirmó/contó/comentó/explicó a Pedro: "Cuando yo era pequeño, no me gustaba jugar a las escondidas".

   c. Flavio/él le dijo/afirmó/recordó/aseguró/explicó a Norma: "Si quieres conseguir algo, debes luchar por eso".

   d. Flavio/él le dijo/comentó/contó/explicó a Lidia: "Mañana iré a pescar con mi suegro, esperamos que esté soleado."

   e. Flavio/él le dijo/preguntó a Santiago: ¿Quieres venir a mi casa a cenar mañana?

2.

   a. Milagros rápidamente le aseguró a Gonzalo que todo iría bien.

   b. Milagros le contó efusivamente a Daniela que Mariana y Darío están/estaban saliendo. (Podría ir en presente si Mariana y Darío continúan saliendo en el presente)

   c. Milagros le preguntó a Fabiana enfáticamente a qué hora quería salir mañana/el día siguiente.

   d. Milagros le comentó a Bruno que desgraciadamente debía trabajar el lunes/ese lunes.

   e. Milagros le pidió a Clara que le prestara un lápiz.

3.

   a. Lo de que

   b. Lo que

   c. Lo de

   d. Lo que

   e. Lo de

4.
   a. Parece
   b. al parecer
   c. De alguna manera
   d. Al parecer

5.
   a. ¿todavía no entregaste la tarea?
   b. pura
   c. y eso
   d. ¿entiendes?
   e. ¿y qué pasó?

6.
   a. ii. ¿No había nadie en casa?
   b. i. ¿De Juan?
   c. iii. ¿Felicia salió?

7.
   a. iii. ¡Pero si son todos médicos!
   b. ii. ¿Graciela se cayó?
   c. i. ¡Pero si siempre fueron mejores amigos!

8.
   a. No, no eran las 11 de la mañana (cuando se levantó) eran las 10.
   b. No, no se bañó ni desayunó antes de salir. Solo se cambió.
   c. No, no fue en bicicleta (en lo que fue) al trabajo. Fue en taxi.
   d. No, no fue su secretaria (quien la regañó). (Quien la regañó) fue su jefe.

9.
   a. de ahí que
   b. Por ello
   c. pues

      d. así que

10.

      a. En un café.

      b. Que su aniversario sería el fin de semana siguiente.

      c. ii. Expresar sorpresa

      d. Le preguntó: "¿Ocurre algo?"

Chapter 4: Protecting the Environment

Quien planta árboles está al lado de la eternidad. Nuestra codicia legítima de más bosques es la búsqueda de una humanidad más humana.

- Joaquín Araújo

In this chapter, we'll give you a repertoire of vocabulary, expressions and phrases to talk about the environment.

Words and Expressions to Talk About Nature and Landscapes

Words that appear together when we talk about nature

Adjectives and expressions to talk about **la tierra** ("the land"):

- *Rica*: rich
- *Fértil*: fertile
- *Desértica*: barren
- *Árida*: arid
- *Estéril*: barren

Adjectives and expressions to talk about **la zona** ("the area"):

- *Sísmica*: seismic
- *Peligrosa*: dangerous
- *Húmeda*: wet

- *Protegida*: protected
- *Marítima*: maritime
- *Fértil*: fertile
- *Pantanosa*: swampy
- *Boscosa*: wooded
- *Rural*: rural
- *Tropical*: tropical
- *Andina*: Andean

Adjectives and expressions to talk about **el cielo** ("the sky"):

- *Azul*: blue
- *Claro*: clear
- *Nublado*: cloudy
- *Despejado*: cloudless
- *Transparente*: transparent
- *Gris*: leaden (grayish color)
- *Tormentoso*: stormy

Adjectives and expressions to talk about **la catástrofe** ("the catastrophe"):

- *Natural*: natural
- *Medioambiental*: environmental
- *Inminente*: impending
- *Ecológica*: ecological
- *Irreparable*: irreparable
- *Humanitaria*: humanitarian
- *Climática*: climate

Adjectives and expressions to talk about **el sitio** ("the location"):

- *Volcánico*: volcanic
- *Desértico*: desert

- *Silvestre*: wild
- *Inhóspito*: inhospitable
- *Rural*: rural
- *Llano*: flat

Adjectives and expressions to talk about **el clima** ("the weather"):

- *Tranquilo*: calm
- *Húmedo*: humid
- *Fértil*: fertile
- *Bueno*: good
- *Abrasador*: scorching
- *Inestable*: unsteady
- *Lluvioso*: rainy
- *Hostil*: hostile
- *Seco*: dry
- *Favorable*: good

Adjectives and expressions to talk about **el volcán** ("the volcano"):

- *En erupción*: erupting
- *Activo*: active
- *Dormido*: sleeping
- *Extinto*: extinct
- *Humeante*: smoky

Adjectives and expressions to talk about **la placa** ("the plate"):

- *Tectónica*: tectonic
- *En movimiento*: moving

Literary resources

- *Personificación*. This resource consists in giving human qualities to things or animals, making them talk, act or react as if they were people. For example: *Una masa de nubes negras miraba desde arriba.* ("A mass of black clouds watched from above.")

- *Símil.* It consists of comparing a real element with another similar one. We normally construct this resource with the following words and expressions: *como, tal como, igual que.* For example: *el cielo de Bariloche se tiñó de un gris como el plomo.* ("...the sky was tinted of a lead-gray color.")

- *Metáfora.* It is a type of analogy or association between elements that share a similar meaning to substitute one with the other. *For example: la ciudad volvió a ver el sol.* ("...the city saw the sun again.")

Vocabulary Related to Pollution and the Environment

Let's see some more vocabulary needed to talk about pollution:

- *Hora pico*: rush hour
- *Tráfico vehicular*: traffic jam
- *Partículas en suspensión*: suspended particulate matter
- *Nube de esmog*: smog cloud
- *Enfermarse*: to get sick
- *Vías respiratorias*: respiratory tracts
- *Calidad del aire*: air quality
- *Contaminación atmosférica*: air pollution
- *Vehículos viejos*: old vehicles
- *Compensación económica*: economic compensation
- *Vehículo más ecológico*: greener vehicle
- *Camiones*: trucks
- *Gas de efecto invernadero*: greenhouse gas
- *Sin emisiones/Emisiones cero*: zero emission
- *Mejora de calidad del aire*: improvement in air quality

- *Sustancias nocivas*: toxic topics
- *Gestión medioambiental*: environmental management
- *Disminuir*: to reduce

Concessive clauses

In this section, we'll delve into concessive sentences.

Aunque

Concessive sentences usually consist of two parts. The subordinate clause (underlined in the examples below) is introduced by a concessive linking word, like *aunque*. In it, we express an unfavorable circumstance or an obstacle to what is said in the main clause, which tends to be an affirmative statement, but it can also be a question or an invitation. Let's take a look at some examples:

- *Aunque no haga la diferencia, yo seguiré reciclando los residuos.* ("Even if it doesn't make any difference, I'll continue to recycle.")
- *Aunque quizá ya lo dijo, ¿qué opina de los incendios en la selva amazónica?* ("Although you may have already said it, what do you think of the fires in the Amazon rainforest?")
- *Aunque a lo mejor ya fuiste parte de una ONG, aquí te dejo un folleto para que veas lo que hacemos en Greenpeace.* ("Although you may already take part in an NGO, here's a leaflet for you to see what we do in Greenpeace.")

Choosing tense and mood

Aunque is one of the most frequent concessive linking words. It can be used both with verbs in the indicative and in the subjunctive moods, to express different nuances. With the structure *aunque + presente del indicativo* we present the concession in the subordinate clause as a real situation.

Page | 69

- *Aunque el gobierno dice que harán algo para evitar la tala ilegal, yo no les creo.* ("Despite the government is saying they'll do something to prevent indiscriminate logging, I don't believe them." The Government is actually saying it)

We use the structure *aunque + presente del subjuntivo* when we cannot state if the concession is real, or when it's not necessary to state it, because we present it as something known.

- *Aunque el Gobierno diga que hará algo, yo no les creo.* ("Despite the Government saying they'll do something, I don't believe them." I don't know or it's not relevant whether the government says it or not.)

We use *aunque + imperfecto de subjuntivo* to present the concession as an improbable situation in the future, or unreal in the present.

- *Aunque el gobierno dijera algo, yo no les creería.* ("Even if the government said something, I wouldn't believe them." I don't believe the government is going to say something.)

Lastly, we use *aunque + pluscuamperfecto del subjuntivo* to talk about unreal past concessions.

- *Aunque el gobierno hubiera dicho algo, no les hubiera creído.* ("Even if the government had said something, I wouldn't have believed them." the government didn't say anything)

Uses of Prepositions *por* and *para*

Let's take some time to think about two very used prepositions in Spanish. *Por* and *para* have similar meanings, but we use them in different cases.

Referring to location

por + *lugar* expresses and approximate location.

- *Mi hermano está por Barcelona.* ("My brother is around Barcelona.")

por + *lugar* expresses the trajectory of a real or figurative movement.

- *Se trabó la puerta, así que tuvimos que salir por la ventana.* ("The door was stuck, so we had to leave through the window.")

para + *lugar* expresses direction.

- *Mi hermano se va para Barcelona mañana.* ("My brother is leaving for Barcelona tomorrow.")

Referring to time

por + *parte del día* is used to place an event in a part of the day.

- *Mañana por la tarde, se manifestarán en contra de la contaminación.* ("Tomorrow afternoon, they will demonstrate against pollution.")

para + *momento* is used to express the proper time for something.

- *Están haciendo pancartas para mañana.* ("They are doing banners for tomorrow.")

Referring to cause

porque/por + *infinitivo/sustantivo/pronombre* is used to express cause.

- *La compañía no cumple con los requisitos medioambientales. Por eso van a protestar mañana.* ("The company does not comply with environmental requirements. That's why they are protesting tomorrow.")

- *Van a protestar mañana porque la compañía no cumple con los requisitos medioambientales.* ("They are protesting tomorrow because the company does not comply with environmental requirements.")

para + que/infinitivo/sustantivo/pronombre is used to express motive: a subsequent situation that we want to achieve through action,

- *El Gobierno tenía que decidir qué hacer con el derrame de petróleo. Para eso consultó a los expertos.* ("Government had to decide what to do about the oil spill. That's why the consulted the experts.")
- *El Gobierno consultó a los expertos para decidir qué hacer con el derrame de petróleo.* ("Government consulted the experts because they had to decide what to do about the oil spill.")

para + sustantivo/infinitivo, oración principal is used to express a concession on what's being stated in the main sentence.

- *Para haber hecho campaña con los ecologistas, el partido gobernante ha hecho poco por el medioambiente.* ("Despite having run the campaign together with the ecologists, the ruling party has done little for the environment.")

Referring to people

por + sustantivo de persona is used to reveal the agent, the person doing the action.

- *Los incendios fueron causados por los dueños de los campos.* ("The fires were started by the owners of the fields.")

por + *pronombre personal* is used to express how an action affects us.

- *Por él se puede prender fuego toda la región. No le importa en lo más mínimo.* ("As far as he's concerned, the whole region can catch fire. He couldn't care less.")

hacer algo por alguien expresses that someone does something for someone else.

- *Las ONG están haciendo el trabajo sucio por el gobierno* (NGOs are doing the government's dirty job.)

para + *sustantivo de persona* is used to reveal the recipient of an action.

- *Esas leyes fueron redactadas para los CEO.* (Those laws were written for the CEOs.)

para + *pronombre personal* is used to introduce an opinion.

- *Para mí, lo que está sucediendo en el Amazonas es el desastre ambiental más grande del último siglo.* ("For me, what's happening in the Amazon rainforest is the biggest environmental disaster of the last century.")

Referring to objects

sustantivo + *por* + *infinitivo* is used to express that the action of the infinitive (which has to be done on the object) is pending.

- *Todavía hay muchas cosas por hacer respecto al medio ambiente.* ("There's still a lot to be done regarding the environment.")

sustantivo + para + infinitivo expresses that the object is used for the action of the infinitive.

- Compraron *camiones de bomberos para combatir los incendios.* ("They bought fire trucks to fight the fires.")

Other uses

sustantivo cuantificado + por + sustantivo is used to express that the magnitude of the first element depends on the second.

- *Dos veces por año, la asamblea vota a sus representantes.* (Twice a year, the convention votes its representatives.)

Talking About Rights and Responsibilities

. Let's take a look at all the things that citizens and governments do with laws:

- *promulgar una ley* ("to enact a law")
- *cumplir la ley* ("to follow the law")
- *aprobar una ley* ("to pass a law")
- *la ley establece que...* ("The law establishes that...")
- *entrar en vigor/vigencia* ("to become effective")
- *estar en vigor/vigencia* ("to be in force")
- *revocar una ley* ("to repeal")

Now, let's take a look at some more common collocations that will come in handy when talking about the law and government responsibilities.

- ***Cumplir con*** + *las tareas, las instrucciones y requerimientos, las exigencias, las expectativas* ("To comply with + the tasks, the instructions and requirements, the demands, the expectations").

- **_Garantizar_** + _el ejercicio de los derechos, el cumplimiento de la ley, los servicios básicos_ ("To guarantee + the exercise of rights, the law enforcement, basic services").
- **_Acceder a_** + _los datos, la información, al archivo_ ("To access + the data, the information, the file").
- **_Velar por_** + _el cumplimiento de las normas, la seguridad de los ciudadanos, los derechos del consumidor_ ("To watch over + the observance of the norms, the safety of the citizens, consumers rights").
- **_Solicitar_** + _la revisión del acuerdo_ ("To ask for + the revision of the agreement").
- **_Respetar_** + _el acuerdo firmado, el trato, los derechos_ ("To respect + the agreement signed, the deal, the rights").
- **_Hacer_** + _una denuncia, una demanda, una consulta, una queja_ ("To file + a report, a demand, a request, a complaint").
- **_Tramitar_** + _una consulta, una solicitud_ ("To process + a query, an application").

Exercises

1. Read the following sentences and fill in the gaps with the corresponding letter.
    a. La cena fue preparada por mi hijo.
    b. La cena fue preparada para mi hijo.
       En .... el hijo es el agasajado con la cena; en .... el hijo es quien agasaja preparando la cena.
    c. Para eso me quedaba en casa.
    d. Por eso me quedaba en casa.
       En .... explico la razón de quedarme en casa; en .... doy a entender que quedarme en casa hubiera sido una mejor opción.
    e. Por él, haz un sándwich.
    f. Para él, haz un sándwich.
       En .... a él le parece bien que le preparen un sandwich; en .... pide un sándwich.
    g. Por la edad que tiene, se mueve muy bien.
    h. Para la edad que tiene, se mueve muy bien.
       En .... no le dio importancia a la edad; en .... la edad es el motivo de moverse bien.

2. Connect the items from column A with the ones in column B.

A	B
a. Promulgar una ley	i. Lo hacen o deben hacerlo los ciudadanos, las empresas, las instituciones, etc.
b. Cumplir la ley	ii. Hacer público que se ha aprobado una ley

c. Aprobar una ley	iii. Sucede una vez se aprueba y es decretado por el Jefe de Estado
d. Establecer (la ley establece que...)	ix. Ordenar lo que se debe hacer
e. Entrar en vigor/vigencia	x. Anular
f. Estar en vigor/vigencia	xi. Cuando el parlamento acepta una ley
g. Revocar una ley	xii. Estar vigente

3. Fill in the gaps with a word from the box:

rural - dormido/a - fértil - despejado/a - húmedo/a - inestable - inminente

    a. Decimos que la tierra es .... cuando es muy productiva y crece en ella lo que se planta.

    b. Una zona .... se caracteriza por tener abundantes lluvias.

    c. El cielo está .... cuando no hay nubes en él.

    d. Una catástrofe .... es una que está por suceder pronto.

    e. Decimos que una locación es .... cuando está en el campo, alejado de la ciudad.

    f. El clima está .... cuando hay peligro de que cambie de un momento a otro.

    g. Un volcán .... puede entrar en actividad esporádicamente.

4. Decide if the following bolded literary resources are *un símil*, *una metáfora*, or *una personificación*.
   a. Los pobladores veían cómo **las llamas de fuego** consumían el tan querido bosque.
   b. Habían perdido todas las esperanzas. Pero **la naturaleza es sabia** y, luego de tres días de incendios continuos, se largó una lluvia torrencial.
   c. Cuando se apagó el fuego, los pobladores regresaron al bosque y lo encontraron **desolado como un desierto**.

5. Use the vocabulary you've learnt in this chapter to fill in the gaps.
   a. El Estado ofrece una .... a todo aquel que sustituya su vehículo viejo por otro más ecológico.
   b. Eso contribuye a una mejora notable de la .... en la ciudad.
   c. El día de ayer, tuvo lugar una concurrida .... en contra de la construcción de la carretera interurbana.
   d. El esmog que sobrevuela la ciudad tiene consecuencias negativas en las ....
   e. La .... dificulta la realización de deportes al aire libre.

6. For each sentence below, decide if the concession in the subordinate clause is a real situation (i); if we cannot state if it's real or not (ii); if it's an improbable situation in the future (iii); or if it's an unreal past concession (ix).
   a. Aunque el CEO de la empresa petrolera la convoque a una reunión, la líder de la agrupación ecologista no asistirá.

b. Aunque el CEO de la empresa petrolera la hubiera convocado a una reunión, la líder de la agrupación ecologista no hubiera asistido.
c. Aunque el CEO de la empresa petrolera la convocó a una reunión, la líder de la agrupación ecologista no asistirá.
d. Aunque el CEO de la empresa petrolera la convocara a una reunión, la líder de la agrupación ecologista no asistiría.

7. Fill in the gaps with one of the concessive structures we've seen in this chapter. Use a different one for each sentence.
   a. .... la contaminación ha dejado de aumentar, sigue siendo alarmante.
   b. .... las ONG hacen muchísimo para defender el medioambiente, sin la ayuda de los gobiernos es imposible lograr un cambio real.
   c. .... haber prometido disminuir los gases de efecto invernadero, los países del primer mundo siguen contaminando la atmósfera.
   d. .... el aumento de la cantidad de gente que recicla, en los países del tercer mundo se sigue quemando mucha basura.

8. Choose a verb from the box below, and conjugate it in the right tense to fill in the gaps. More than one option may be correct.

cuidar - ser - reciclar - protestar

   a. Por más plástico que los ciudadanos ...., una gran parte termina en los océanos.
   b. Por mucho que las ONG ...., el Gobierno no va a ceder ante los reclamos.

c. Por más que los consumidores .... los recursos no renovables, la diferencia la hacen las grandes empresas.

d. Por muy orgánica que .... la verdura, siempre tiene algún fertilizante.

9. Rewrite the following sentences using one of the phrases and expressions to judge a situation that we've seen in this chapter:

   a. La sociedad desaprueba que los ministros del Gobierno sean accionistas en empresas petroleras.

   b. No está bien que los peatones y ciclistas tengan que respirar los gases de los coches.

   c. Levantarse de la mesa antes de que todos hayan terminado de comer es una grosería.

   d. Es esperable que los ciudadanos peleen por sus derechos, ¿no?

Answer Key

1. En **b.** el hijo es el agasajado con la cena; en **a.** el hijo es quien agasaja preparando la cena.

   En **b.** explico la razón de quedarme en casa; en **a.** doy a entender que quedarme en casa hubiera sido una mejor opción.

   En **a.** a él le parece bien que le preparen un sandwich; en **b.** pide un sándwich.

   En **b.** no le dio importancia a la edad; en **a.** la edad es el motivo de moverse bien.

2.
   a. ii.
   b. i.
   c. xi.
   d. ix.
   e. iii.
   f. xii.
   g. x.

3. Fill in the gaps with a word from the box:
   a. fértil
   b. húmeda
   c. despejado
   d. inminente
   e. rural
   f. inestable
   g. dormido

4.
   a. una metáfora
   b. una personificación
   c. un simil

5. Use the vocabulary you've learnt in this chapter to fill in the gaps.
   a. compensación económica
   b. calidad del aire
   c. manifestación/protesta
   d. vías respiratorias
   e. contaminación atmosférica

6.
   a. ii.
   b. ix.
   c. i.
   d. iii.

7.
   a. Si bien/A pesar de que/Pese a que
   b. A pesar de que/Si bien/Pese a que
   c. Pese a/A pesar de
   d. A pesar de/Pese a

8.
   a. reciclen/reciclan
   b. protesten
   c. cuiden/cuidan
   d. es/sea

9.
   a. Está mal visto que los ministros del Gobierno sean accionistas en empresas petroleras.
   b. Es injusto que los peatones y ciclistas tengan que respirar los gases de los coches.
   c. Levantarse de la mesa antes de que todos hayan terminado de comer es de mala educación.

d. Es lógico que los ciudadanos peleen por sus derechos, ¿no?

Chapter 5: Online and Offline Relationships

El respeto por los sentimientos ajenos es la mejor condición para una próspera y feliz vida de relaciones y afectos.

- José Saramago

In this chapter, we will talk about relationships online and offline. Are you ready to get passionate about learning Spanish? Let's start!

Vocabulary About Social Media and the Internet

We'll examine some basic nouns used in social media and some verbs and collocations between the nouns and the verbs we've seen.

Let's start with some common nouns!

- *las redes sociales*: social media
- *las redes*: social media
- *la publicación*: post
- *el perfil*: profile
- *seguidores*: followers
- *seguidos*: following
- *la comunidad de seguidores*: community of followers
- *los suscriptores*: subscribers
- *el artículo*: article
- *el me gusta*: like

- *la tendencia*: trending topic
- *el tuit*: tweet
- *el canal*: channel
- *la etiqueta*: tag
- *la solicitud de amistad*: friend request
- *el comentario*: comment
- *el mensaje directo*: the direct message
- *el mensaje*: message
- *la bandeja de entrada*: inbox
- *la notificación*: notification
- *el inicio*: feed
- *el correo no deseado*: spam
- *el filtro*: filter
- *la cámara frontal*: front camera
- *la cámara trasera*: back camera
- *el borrador*: draft

As we know, social media is a huge part of our globalized world and, in some cases, this also makes people use English words in Spanish. For example, "likes" on social media are *me gustas* in Spanish, but Spanish speakers might still talk about "likes" sometimes. However, there are some words that have no Spanish translation, so we always say them in English, even in Spanish! Some examples are: "blog," "vlog," "influencer," "selfie," "stream," "meme," and "hashtag." When Spanish speakers use English words like these ones, they usually try to pronounce them similar to English, but with Spanish vowels and consonants (if that makes any sense!). For example, "stream." One exception is "meme," which is always read in Spanish as MEH-meh.

Now let's see some verbs related to social media and some collocations with the nouns we've seen before!

- *seguir*: to follow

- *compartir*: to share
- *suscribirse*: to subscribe
- *agregar*: to add
- *publicar*: to post
- *etiquetar*: to tag
- *tuitear*: to tweet
- *dar me gusta*: to like
- *ser tendencia*: to be a trending topic
- *tener seguidores*: to have followers
- *bloquear*: to block
- *silenciar*: to silence
- *denunciar*: to report
- *enviar un mensaje*: send a message
- *dejar un comentario*: leave a message
- *editar el perfil*: edit profile
- *programar una publicación/un tuit*: schedule a post/tweet

There are some English words that have gone through changes to turn them into new words that are more similar to Spanish words. Usually, these words are verbs. For example, when we tag someone on one of our posts, in Spanish we might use the word *etiquetar*, but you might also hear the "Spanglish" version *taggear* which makes the verb *tag* into a verb ending in *-ar*. Like *taggear*, you might hear other words like *likear, chatear, bloggear, postear, streamear,* and *stalkear*. And you might be wondering how to read these words. Well, there is no one way. The people who know more English will pronounce them more similarly to English and the people who know less English will pronounce them in Spanish and, of course, there are various ways in the middle.

There are also a few adjectives commonly used in social media. Let's see them and some collocations!

- *viral*: viral
  - *publicación viral*
  - *meme viral*
  - influencer *viral*
- *enviado*: sent
  - *mensaje enviado*
  - *correo enviado*
  - *tuit enviado*
- *recibido*: received
  - *mensaje recibido*
  - *correo recibido*
- *visto*: seen
  - *mensaje visto*
- *suscrito*: subscribed
- *guardado/a*: saved
  - *publicación guardada*

Verbs Used to Talk About Relationships

Whether we're talking about romantic relationships or not, there are some verbs that are useful when we want to describe our relationship with someone or something that someone has done to us. In this section, we will deal with some of those verbs and their collocations.

- *incomodar (a...)*: to get (someone) uncomfortable
- *presentar (a...)*: to introduce (someone)
- *agredir (a...)*: to attack/insult (someone)
- *ofender (a...)*: to offend (someone)
- *enamorarse (de...)*: to fall in love (with...)
- *encariñarse (de...)*: to get attached (to...), to be fond (of...)
- *dejar (a alguien)*: to leave (someone)
- *gustar (alguien)*: to like (someone)

- *pasar de (alguien)*: to not have interest (in someone), despise (someone)
- *seducir (a...)*: to seduce (someone)
- *fascinar*: to fascinate
- *atraer (a...)*: to attract
- *conquistar (a...)*: to win over
- *engañar (a...)*: to cheat
- *persuadir (a...)*: to persuade
- *deslumbrar (a...)*: to dazzle
- *tratar (a alguien) (+ adverbio)*: to treat (someone) (+adverb)
  - *tratar bien (a...)*: to treat someone good
  - *tratar mal (a...)*: to treat someone badly
  - *tratar de igual a igual (a...)*: to treat someone like equals
  - *tratar con cordialidad (a...)*: to treat someone cordially
  - *tratar con amabilidad (a...)*: to treat someone kindly
  - *tratar con frialdad (a...)*: to treat someone coldly
  - *tratar con distancia (a...)*: to be distant (with...)

Some collocations with *tener*:

- *tener (mucho/poco) trato (con...)*: to talk/interact (a lot/little) (with...)
- *tener una relación (+ adjetivo)*: to have a (+ adjective) + relationship
- *tener respeto (a...)*: to have respect for
- *tener cariño (a...)*: to be fond of
- *tener envidia (a...)*: to envy someone
- *tener miedo (a...)*: to be afraid of
- *tener celos (de...)*: to be jealous of
- *tener paciencia (con...)*: to have patience (with...)
- *tener aprecio*: to hold in high esteem/ to have appreciation
- *tener confianza en...*: to confide in

Some collocations with *llevarse*:

- *llevarse bien (con...)*: to get on well (with...)
- *llevarse estupendamente (con...):* to get on great (with...)
- *llevarse mal (con...):* to get on badly (with...)
- *llevarse fatal (con...)*: to get on awful (with...)
- *llevarse como perros y gatos (con...)*: to get on badly, to fight like cats and dogs (with...)

Referring to People

We will see a few ways to refer to people that convey more than simply talking about people. Let's have a look!

De esos/esas and *de estos/estas*

We use the phrases *de esos/esas* and *de estos/estas* to talk about things or people and minimize them. In this way, we talk as if it wasn't important or prestigious. Let's see some examples:

- *Subió un artículo <u>de estos</u> que hablan sobre un restaurante de moda.* ("She uploaded one of those articles that talk about a trendy restaurant.")
- *Es una persona <u>de esas</u> que dicen todo lo que piensan.* ("He's one of those people who say everything they think.")

As you can see, the gender of *esos/esas* and *esto/esta* depends on our subject, which in the first case is *un artículo* and in the second *una persona*. However, the number of *esos/esas* and *estos/estas* is always plural and it shouldn't change because we're generalizing.

Este/esta

When we want to refer to someone with disdain, we might simply refer to them as *este* or *esta*. In Spanish, using this demonstrative in this way reflects that we don't like the person we're talking about. Let's see some examples:

- *Esta se cree la reina del universo.* ("This girl thinks she is the queen of the universe.")
- *¿Y este qué quiere?* ("What does this guy want?")
- *Estas no tienen ni 25 años y ya están dando consejos de vida.* ("This girl isn't even 25 and she's already giving life advice.")
- *Estos se creen que por ser hijos del dueño son dueños de nosotros.* ("These guys think that because they are the owners' sons they own us.")

Este and *esta* agree in gender and number with the person or people we are talking about. Our interlocutor usually knows who we're referring to based on context. Remember, that these demonstratives are used only when we want to say something mean or hurtful.

Un/una tal

We can also use the demonstrative *tal* to talk about people. We can also use it to express that we don't know the person we're talking about. Let's see examples of this:

- *Mi nueva compañera es una tal Alejandra Ríos, ¿la conoces?* ("My new partner is somebody named Alejandra Ríos, do you know her?")
- *Un tal Andrés vino a buscarte.* ("Someone named Andrés came looking for you.")

The indefinite article changes according to the gender of the person we're talking about, but the demonstrative *tal* doesn't change.

We can also use this in the plural with *unos tales* and *unas tales*, but this isn't actually common. We generally use this structure to talk about one person.

Let's now see an example using the vocabulary, the verbs and the resources to refer to people we've seen so far. This is a chat conversation between Julián (•) and Lucía (○). Let's have a look:

• Camila publicó uno de esos videos en los que muchas personas bailan la misma canción. Lo has visto?

○ No, muéstramelo.
○ Esa se cree que es mejor que todos, no?

• Ay, sí. Hace todos los videos que están en tendencia para obtener más me gustas.

○ Yo paso de ella.
○ Ya no la sigo ni interactúo mucho con ella.

• Yo me llevo fatal con ella y también le tengo un poco de envidia.

○ Envidia?
○ Y eso por qué?

• Porque tiene muchísimos seguidores y uno de sus videos se hizo viral hace poco.
• Es casi famosa!

        ○ Tú también puedes serlo si
               quieres.

● Tú crees?

● El otro día me contactó un
tal Jeremías para que hiciera
unas publicidades, pero no sé
si las haré.

        ○ Hazlas! Es tu sueño.

● Sí, puede ser...

Note that when we're texting in Spanish we usually leave out the opening question and exclamation marks.

Suffixes

Suffixes are morphemes that are added to the end of words to form a different word. For example, in Spanish, an adverb like *rápidamente* is actually the adjective *rápido/a* followed by the suffix *-mente*, like we've seen before.

In this case, however, we're not going to form adverbs but adjectives. We'll start with adjectives formed by a verb followed by the suffix *-ble*. Let's see a few examples!

- *creer → creíble* ("believable")
- *aceptar → aceptable* ("acceptable")
- *presentar → presentable* ("presentable")
- *cuestionar → cuestionable* ("cuestionable")
- *influenciar → influenciable* ("impressionable")
- *manipular → manipulable* ("manipulable")
- *envidiar → envidiable* ("enviable")
- *confiar → confiable* ("reliable")
- *amigar/socializar → amigable/sociable* ("friendly", "sociable")

As you can see, the Spanish versions of these adjectives are really similar to the Spanish ones, so you might already guess what this suffix means. Basically, the adjectives ending in *-ble* indicate that the person or thing is capable of receiving the action expressed by the verb. Let's take an example. *Creer* means "to believe," and *creíble* means that the thing or person can be believed.

Note that since these adjectives end in *-e*, you don't need to change them to make them agree in gender and number with the subject!

But *-ble* isn't the only suffix we'll see here! We will now learn about a few others!

We can add the suffixes *-ete/eta, -ón/ona, -ote/ota,* and *-azo/aza* to some adjectives and nouns to give them a slightly different meaning. Let's see those meanings with some examples!

- *-ete/eta*: When we add *-ete/eta* to nouns or adjectives, we add a sense of sympathy or complicity. In some cases it is used in a derogatory way too, depending on the word intensifies its meaning.
  - *amigo/a → el amiguete/a*
  - *viejo/a → el vejete/a*
  - *majo/a → majete/a*
- *-ón/ona*: If we add *-ón/ona* to nouns or adjectives instead, we intensify their meaning, whether it is positive or negative.
  - *simple → simplón/ona*
  - *la película → el peliculón*
  - *el drama → el dramón*
  - *el problema → el problemón*
- *-ote/ota*: If we add *-ote/ota* to nouns or adjectives, we add a nuance of sympathy while intensifying their meaning.
  - *grande → grandote/a*

- *feo/a → feote/a*
    - *raro/a → rarote/a*
- -*azo/aza*: If we add -*azo/aza* to a noun (not an adjective), we are saying something positive about their quality or size.
    - *el cuerpo → el cuerpazo*
    - *el pelo → el pelazo*
    - *artista → el/la artistazo/a*

Lo que más/menos

In romantic or non-romantic relationships, we might want to say what we like the most or the least about someone, and for that we use *lo que más* and *lo que menos*. Let's start with a simple example:

<u>Lo que menos</u> <u>me gusta</u> *de Lorenzo es su desorganización.* ("What I like the least about Lorenzo is his disorganization")

To form these sentences, we should first write *lo que más* or *lo que menos* and then a verb. Of course, to talk about what we like or dislike, we would normally use verbs like *gustar, encantar, amar, odiar,* etc. But there are many other verbs we can use to convey different things, like *disfrutar, emocionar, querer, lamentar,* among others. After the verb, if we are talking about someone, we should add the preposition *de* and the name or pronoun of the person we're talking about.

Let's see a few other examples:

- *Lo que más disfruto de mis hijos es compartir tiempo con ellos.* ("What I enjoy the most about my children is sharing time with them.")
- *Lo que más odio de Guillermo es su impuntualidad.* ("What I hate the most about Guillermo is his tardiness.")
- *Lo que más quiero en esta vida es que León se case conmigo.* ("What I want the most in this life is for León to marry me.")

Como si + imperfecto/pluscuamperfecto de subjuntivo

We use the structure *como si + pretérito imperfecto/pluscuamperfecto de subjuntivo* to describe a situation while comparing it with another hypothetical situation. Do you remember how to form these two tenses? Well, in case you don't, let's see their regular conjugations with the verbs *cantar, comer,* and *vivir.*

Pretérito imperfecto de subjuntivo:

	Cantar	Comer	Vivir
yo	cantara / cantase	comiera / comiese	viviera / viviese
tú	cantaras / cantases	comieras / comieses	vivieras / vivieses
él / ella / usted	cantara / cantase	comiera /comiese	viviera / viviese
nosotros / nosotras	cantáramos / cantásemos	comiéramos / comiésemos	viviéramos / viviésemos
vosotros / vosotras	cantarais / cantaseis	comierais / comieseis	vivierais / viviésemos
ellos / ellas / ustedes	cantaran / cantasen	comieran / comiesen	vivieran / viviesen

Pretérito pluscuamperfecto de subjuntivo:

	Auxiliar	Participio

yo	hubiera / hubiese	
tú	hubieras / hubieses	
él / ella / usted	hubiera / hubiese	cantado
nosotros / nosotras	hubiéramos / hubiésemos	comido vivido
vosotros / vosotras	hubierais / hubieseis	
ellos / ellas / ustedes	hubieran / hubiesen	

Just like with conditional sentences, we use the imperfect subjunctive to talk about situations that haven't finished. For example: *"Ahora mi novio me trata como si fuera una princesa"* ("Now my boyfriend treats me like a princess"), or *"En ese momento, mi novio me trató como si fuera una princesa"* ("At that time, my boyfriend treated me like a princess").

On the other hand, we can use the *pretérito pluscuamperfecto de subjuntivo* to talk about situations that have ended. For example: *"Mi novio me trata como si hubiera hecho algo malo"* ("My boyfriend treats me as if I had done something wrong").

And we can also use it independently to answer something that we think is inappropriate. For example, if a colleague orders us: *"Entrega todo para mañana"* ("Hand in everything by tomorrow"), we could answer: ¡*Como si tú fueras el jefe!* ("As if you were the boss!")

Let's have a look at the following conversation between Germán (●) and Luisa (○):

● ¿Has visto la última película de Netflix?

○ Sí, me pareció un peliculón.

● ¿De veras? A mí no me gustó mucho.

○ Bueno, ella me parece una artistaza y ¿has visto su cuerpazo? Y él parece majete.

● Sí, pero a mí su relación me pareció poco creíble. Se tratan como si todo estuviera bien. Y luego de que ocurre el crimen actúan como si no hubiera pasado nada. Es extraño, ¿no?

○ Sí, puede ser, pero a mí me encantó. Lo que más me encantó fue la escena de terror.

● Ah, eso sí estuvo bueno, pero lo que menos disfruté fue la relación entre ellos.

○ ¡Como si tú fueras el rey de las relaciones!

Exercises

1. Fill in the gaps with the words from the box to make some collocations related to social media and the internet.

> social - amistad - comentarios - seguidores - directos - perfil - entrada

   a. Quiero editar mi .... y poner una foto nueva. ¿Me tomas una?
   b. A esta *influencer* le dejaron muchos .... en su última publicación.
   c. Tengo la bandeja de .... llena de mensajes .... de gente que no conozco.
   d. La comunidad de .... de esta *influencer* agotó todos los productos en segundos.
   e. Mi madre me envió una solicitud de .... por Facebook. ¿No sabe que esa red .... ya casi no se usa?

2. Read the following sentences and then determine if the sentence below it is true (T) or false (F).
   a. Javier engañó a Laura y luego la dejó.
      i. Laura cheated on Javier.
   b. Miranda deslumbró a todo el mundo con su increíble actuación.
      i. Miranda acted so incredibly that everyone was dazzled.
   c. Luis se encariñó con el hijo de Paola.
      i. Luis didn't get on well with Paola's son.
   d. Juan Carlos sedujo a María y ahora ella está enamorada.
      i. Juan Carlos made María feel uncomfortable, but now she's in love.

e. Francisco no se lleva bien con su hermana y se tratan con frialdad.

     i.   Francisco and his sister are distant and don't treat each other kindly.

3. Fill in the gaps with *de esos, de esas, este, esta, un tal,* or *una tal* where appropriate.
   a. ¿Quién se cree que es ....? Hasta ayer solo era la hermanita de Luis y ahora se cree que es mejor que el resto.
   b. Él es .... que niegan el calentamiento global.
   c. Te llamó .... "Pocho" o "Polo". Dijo que lo llamaras.
   d. No soy .... que prometen cosas y luego no las cumplen.
   e. .... Sandra Ramos quiere hablar contigo. ¿Quién es?
   f. .... se pasea por la fábrica como si fuera el dueño.

4. Form adjectives from the following verbs by adding the suffix -*ble*. What do the adjectives mean?
   a. Manejar
   b. Tratar
   c. Odiar
   d. Adorar
   e. Variar

5. Match the following words with the meaning that their suffixes convey:

   a. problemón

b. rarote

c. vejete

d. pelazo

   i.   Conveys a nuance of sympathy and intensified meaning

   ii.   Conveys something positive about the quality or size

  iii. Conveys a sense of sympathy or complicity and intensified meaning

6. Intensifies its positive or negative meaningFill in the gaps with the phrases *lo que más* or *lo que menos* and the present first person singular conjugation of the verbs from the box.

> disfrutar - querer - lamentar - encantar - desear

   a. .... de nuestra relación es que podamos ser sinceros.

   b. .... en esta vida es ser millonario y no tener que trabajar más.

   c. .... de estudiar en la universidad es tomar exámenes, me pongo muy nervioso.

   d. .... en este mundo es que mis hijos sufran.

   e. .... es haberte hecho sentir mal cuando discutimos.

7. Fill in the gaps with the *pretérito imperfecto de subjuntivo* form of the verbs in brackets.

   a. Cada vez que voy a la casa de mi abuela, ella me da de comer como si yo.......................... (estar) muerta de hambre.

   b. A veces, la madre de Jorge lo sigue tratando como si aún .... (ser) un niño pequeño.

   c. Nos duelen las rodillas como si .... (haberse) golpeado.

d. Vosotras actuáis como si .... (querer) ser amigas de todo el mundo.

8. Fill in the gaps with the *pretérito pluscuamperfecto* form of the verbs in brackets.
   a. ¿Estás bien? Te ves como si te .... (chocar) un camión.
   b. ¿Pasó algo? Todos actúan como si .... (ver) un fantasma.
   c. Ayer fuimos a hacer unas compras y el dueño del supermercado me vigilaba como si .... (robar) algo.
   d. Creo que no le caemos bien a los vecinos. Hoy me miraron como si .... (hacer) ruido toda la noche.

9. Fill in the gaps with the *pretérito imperfecto de subjuntivo* or the *pretérito pluscuamperfecto de subjuntivo* form of the verbs in the box.

estar - ser - cantar - gritar - pelearse

   a. Hoy Mateo me está tratando mal, como si anoche ....
   b. Hay unos pájaros en mi ventana que pían como si .... una canción.
   c. Es pleno verano, pero yo tengo frío como si .... nevando.
   d. Me duele la garganta como si .... todo el día ayer, pero estuve en mi casa todo el día.
   e. Sandra perdió su cartera y me mira como si .... mi culpa que la haya dejado en el bar.

10. Read the following text about Magdalena's friend and answer the questions below.

Mi amiga comenzó a hacer videos para YouTube y a llenar su instagram de fotos y publicaciones sobre el cuidado de la piel. En muy poco tiempo, comenzó a ganar seguidores, y en menos de un año ya tenía una gran comunidad de seguidores. Hace poco, hizo una de esas publicaciones sobre un producto nuevo que se hizo viral y ganó miles de seguidores más. Me fascina la interacción que tiene con su comunidad de seguidores porque compran todo lo que ella recomienda como si fuera una gurú, creo que son muy influenciables. Sin embargo, lo que menos le gusta a ella es que, como siempre, hay gente que la critica y la hace sentir incómoda.

    a. ¿Qué consiguió en menos de un año?
- i. Patrocinadores.
- ii. Ser modelo de diferentes marcas.
- iii. Una gran comunidad de seguidores.

    b. ¿Sobre qué era la publicación que se hizo viral?
- i. Un producto nuevo.
- ii. Sobre ella.
- iii. Un baile nuevo.

    c. ¿Qué cree Magdalena de la comunidad de seguidores de su amiga?
- i. Que son fascinantes.
- ii. Que la quieren mucho.
- iii. Que son influenciables.

    d. ¿Qué es lo que menos le gusta a la amiga de Magdalena?
- i. La gente que la reconoce en la calle.
- ii. La gente que la critica.
- iii. Los productos que recibe.

Answer Key

1.

   a. Quiero editar mi <u>perfil</u> y poner una foto nueva. ¿Me tomas una?

   b. A esta *influencer* le dejaron muchos <u>comentarios</u> en su última publicación.

   c. Tengo la bandeja de <u>entrada</u> llena de mensajes <u>directos</u> de gente que no conozco.

   d. La comunidad de <u>seguidores</u> de esta *influencer* agotó todos los productos en segundos.

   e. Mi madre me envió una solicitud de <u>amistad</u> por Facebook. ¿No sabe que esa red <u>social</u> ya casi no se usa?

2.

   a. F
   b. T
   c. F
   d. F
   e. T

3.

   a. esta
   b. de esos
   c. un tal
   d. de esos
   e. Una tal
   f. Este

4.

   a. Manejable: que se puede manejar
   b. Tratable: que se puede tratar
   c. Odiable: que se puede odiar
   d. Adorable: que se puede adorar
   e. Variable: que puede variar

5.

    a. problemón - v. Intensifies its positive or negative meaning

    b. rarote - i. Nuance of sympathy in some cases (not in this one) and intensified meaning

    c. vejete - iii. Sense of sympathy in some cases (not in this one) or complicity and intensified meaning

    d. pelazo - ii. Something positive about the quality or size

6.

    a. Lo que más me encanta
    b. Lo que más deseo
    c. Lo que menos disfruto
    d. Lo que menos quiero
    e. Lo que más lamento

7.

    a. estuviera/estuviese
    b. fuera/fuese
    c. nos hubiéramos/hubiésemos sido golpeados
    d. quisierais/quisieseis

8.

    a. hubiera/hubiese chocado
    b. hubieran/hubiesen visto
    c. hubiera/hubiese robado
    d. hubiéramos hecho/hubiésemos hecho

9.

    a. nos hubiéramos peleado
    b. cantaran
    c. estuviera
    d. hubiera gritado
    e. hubiera sido

10.

a. iii. Una gran comunidad de seguidores.
b. i. Un producto nuevo.
c. iii. Que son influenciables.
d. Ii. La gente que la critica.

Conclusion

We did it! You are now an advanced student of Spanish! In this book, you've learned everything you needed to go from intermediate to advanced in only 30 days. What an accomplishment!

This book was full of vocabulary, grammar, examples, exercises and reading material related to various topics and you've successfully gone through it all and came out the other side victorious!

We hope that you've enjoyed the last thirty days, and remember that you can always come back to this book for tips, to refresh your memory and practice with the exercises again. We're here for you!

We wish you all the best in your next Spanish-learning steps and hope you keep up the great work you've done here with us. *¡Adiós!*

Made in the USA
Las Vegas, NV
03 February 2024

85211657R00066